LANGUAGE, SAUSSURE AND WITTGENSTEIN

How to play games with words

ROUTLEDGE HISTORY OF LINGUISTIC THOUGHT SERIES

The long and complex history of linguistic thought and the importance of the relation between ideas about the nature of language and their social, intellectual and cultural contexts have become a major concern not only for linguists, but also for philosophers, anthropologists, literary theorists and political and social historians. Linguistic historiography reveals that most of the puzzling problems now facing linguists have already surfaced at some time during the more than two millenia of linguistic thought, and that there is a great deal for present-day linguists to learn from the debates of their predecessors.

The Editor and the Publishers wish to draw this Series to the attention of scholars whose concerns mesh language with the history of ideas, and to invite them to submit manuscripts or book-proposals to Professor Talbot J. Taylor, Department of English, College of William and Mary, Williamsburg, Virginia, 23185, USA; or to Jonathan Price, Linguistics Editor, Routledge Publishers, 11 New Fetter Lane, London, EC4P 4EE, UK.

Series Editor
Talbot J. Taylor, College of William and Mary, Williamsburg

OTHER BOOKS IN THE SERIES

Landmarks in Linguistic Thought: The Western Tradition from Socrates to Saussure
Roy Harris and Talbot J. Taylor

Language, Man and Knowledge
Hans Aarsleff

Language, Saussure and Wittgenstein

How to play games with words

Roy Harris

London and New York

First published in hardback in 1988
First published in paperback in 1990
by Routledge
11 New Fetter Lane, London EC4P 4EE
29 West 35th Street, New York NY 10001
Reprinted 1989, 1991

Printed and bound in Great Britain by
T.J. Press (Padstow) Ltd., Padstow, Cornwall

British Library Cataloguing in Publication Data

Harris, Roy
    Language, Saussure and Wittgenstein: how
    to play games with words.
    1. Wittgenstein, Ludwig 2. Languages
    — Philosophy 3. Saussure, Ferdinand de
    Title
    409'.2'4 B3376.W564.L3

Library of Congress Cataloging-in-Publication Data
also available

ISBN 0-415-05225-4

Die Sprache ist ein Labyrinth von Wegen
Wittgenstein

C'est la langue qui fait l'unité du langage
Saussure

Contents

Preface

The history of modern linguistics is not the history of new discoveries about previously unknown languages of the world. It is the history of conflicting views as to how we should set about the analysis of language. In that respect it has little in common with the history of geography, or of physiology, or any of the natural sciences.

In the Graeco-Roman world linguistic enquiry had already become divided into three separate branches: logic, rhetoric and grammar. That influential tripartite division was institutionalised in the curriculum of the first universities of Europe. It is a division which has left an indelible mark on all linguistic thought in the Western tradition, right down to the present.

Western scholarship has uniformly tended to accept rather than to challenge this division. However, at various times during the past two thousand years the question of the relationship between logic, rhetoric and grammar has surfaced as an important academic focus of attention. It was at the core of the philosophy of the medieval *modistae*. It was also crucial to the work of the scholars of Port Royal in the seventeenth century. Today it is once again a key issue in discussions of language. But the way this issue is now addressed in the later decades of the twentieth century differs characteristically from the way it was addressed in earlier periods. This characteristic difference is largely due to the work of two men: Saussure and Wittgenstein.

Both were, in their very different ways, leaders of an intellectual movement which has come to dominate twentieth-century linguistic thought. Both were instrumental in bringing about a radical reassessment of the role played by language in human affairs. The effect of that reassessment may perhaps be summed up as follows. Language is no longer regarded as peripheral to our grasp of the world in which we live, but as central to it. Words are not mere vocal labels or communicational adjuncts superimposed upon an already given order of things. They are collective products of social interaction, essential instruments through which human beings constitute and articulate their world. This typically twentieth-century view of language has profoundly influenced developments throughout the whole range of human sciences. It is particularly marked in linguistics, philosophy, psychology, sociology and anthropology. In all these fields the revolution in linguistic thought which Saussure and Wittgenstein ushered in has yet to run its full course.

The work of each of these thinkers has given rise, understandably, to a formidably large corpus of interpretation, translation, exegesis and criticism. Even to survey this corpus would today require a book of considerable length, and it is no part of the aim of the present writer to undertake such a survey; nor to attempt to trace the complex strands of influence on and influence of Saussure and Wittgenstein. The aim is much more modest and strictly limited in scope. Amid all that has been written on each of these writers, surprisingly little has been devoted to comparison of their views on language. There are various reasons for this. Saussure and Wittgenstein belonged to two very different academic disciplines. Saussure never stressed the implications of his linguistics for philosophy; nor Wittgenstein the implications of his philosophy for linguistics. Each caused a sufficient upheaval within his own discipline to preoccupy commentators with that alone, without prompting cross-disciplinary comparisons. With historical hindsight, however, it now becomes clear that in spite of obvious and fundamental divergences there are also parallels between the two. The positions taken by Saussure and Wittgenstein on linguistic questions, and the problems they encounter as a result, show various similarities. It seems, therefore, worth while briefly to set out what may be seen as the most suggestive points of contact between the linguistic thought of Saussure and of Wittgenstein, leaving as an open question the extent to which these points of contact are significant or deserve further exploration.

In even such a modest venture, needless to say, everything depends on one's readings of the two major figures involved. Comparison cannot be conducted *in vacuo*. At the same time, it would have been impossible here to begin by giving a detailed justification of those readings, since that would have involved exegesis and detailed contextualisation on a scale far beyond the scope of the present book. In the end it seemed better to present the comparative thesis in a fairly bald form and leave it (as Wittgenstein said of language) to speak for itself. The thesis is that the views of Saussure and Wittgenstein show an important convergence which is not commonly acknowledged; specifically in their belief that the most enlightening analogy one can entertain in seeking to understand how language works is the analogy between a language and a rule-governed game. There is no commonly accepted term for this assimilation, which would clearly be out of the question in any society which did not have the institution of games in the sense in which European society recognises chess, tennis, bridge, etc. as games. Given this terminological lacuna, one is reduced to speaking rather vaguely of 'the games analogy' or 'the games perspective'. *The Language Game* might have been a better title for the present book. Its disadvantage is that the notion 'language game' is associated specifically with Wittgenstein, and it might therefore sound as if a Wittgensteinian interpretation is being foisted restrospectively upon Saussure. (Fortunately there is textual evidence in the *Cours* to indicate that this is not the case.)

If history had a hand in any foisting of interpretations it would have been the other way round. It is more than likely that the impact of the later Wittgenstein's philosophy outside the classrooms of professional academic philosophers was in part due to the fact that it came into an intellectual world which had already assimilated the ideas of Saussure. The foregrounding of games in the *Philosophische Untersuchungen* may even have evoked a certain sense of *déjà vu* for readers long familiar with Saussure's favourite metaphor. And outrageous though it might sound in the learned corridors of Wittgensteinian scholarship to whisper that 'the first philosopher of the age' is open to a Saussurean reading, what counts as much in cultural history as what philosophers say is what society perceives them to be saying. Socrates learnt that lesson the hard way on behalf of all his heirs.

Nothing is made in the following chapters of the fact that Saussure and Wittgenstein (neither of them particularly dedicated games-players) lived at a time when Western civilisation was beginning to attribute to games a status they had never previously enjoyed, but which has subsequently gained acceptance as a cultural commonplace throughout the Western world. The significance of this must be left for exploration on another occasion. It involves social and political considerations of the kind which Saussure would have called 'semiological' in the broadest sense; and to have dealt satisfactorily here even with the semiology of games as communication in twentieth-century culture would have meant trying to roll at least two books into one.

In attempting this simple comparison I incur intellectual debts far too numerous to itemise, particularly to colleagues and students for matters raised in the course of discussion. Acknowledgement might in any case conceivably occasion embarrassment, since my use of other people's thinking has been nothing if not eclectic. Saussure and Wittgenstein both provide rich funds of ideas about language, and it is not surprising that their interpretation should often be controversial. I am particularly grateful, however, to Dr Brigitte Nerlich, with whom I held a joint seminar on these two writers at Oxford in 1986, and to Mr S. J. Farrow, whose questions made me think harder. As regards Wittgenstein, what is at issue in these controversies has above all been clarified for me by the recent work of Dr G. P. Baker and Dr P. M. S. Hacker. Both have answered my tedious queries with stoic patience and unfailing courtesy.

Parts of this book were written while I was Visiting Professor at the Jawaharlal Nehru University in New Delhi in 1986. I should like to thank the Vice-Chancellor and Professor H. S. Gill for inviting me to lecture there, and my Indian audiences for their lively participation in exploring some of the linguistic problems which are again touched on here.

Finally, I am grateful to Dr T. J. Taylor for his invitation not only to contribute to but to inaugurate a new series of publications on the history of linguistics. To open with such a controversial topic as the present volume deals with betokens an editor with a refreshingly adventurous view of historiography, long lacking in linguistics. Saussure and Wittgenstein could hardly have been better choices to illustrate the thesis that interpretation and debate are the twin hubs of any historical chariot worth racing.

A Note on Translation

Any discussion in English of the work of Saussure and Wittgenstein poses problems of translation which on bad days do not bear thinking about and to which on good days there is no entirely satisfactory solution. As regards Wittgenstein, I have kept to the text of the published English translations as indicated in the references, even when doubtful about the renderings they give. Passages from Saussure cited in translation are from my own English version (London, 1983). Terms which are recurrently troublesome include, as one might expect, *langage, langue, parole, Sprache* and *Satz*. These five words have been dealt with as follows. Saussure's *langage* is here invariably rendered as 'language', with no accompanying definite or indefinite article in English. Wittgenstein's *Sprache* is variously rendered as 'language' or 'the language': his English translators are not always sensitive to the distinction. Saussure's *langue* is translated as 'the language' or 'a language', occasionally as 'linguistic structure' or 'linguistic system'. *Parole* is invariably translated as 'speech'. German *Satz* is notoriously Janus-faced as regards the notions 'sentence' and 'proposition': again, Wittgenstein's translators do not always seem to choose happily between these alternatives. Renderings of other technical terms are, where appropriate, indicated in the text.

Abbreviations

BB   *Blue and Brown Books*, 2nd edn, R. Rhees (ed.) (Oxford University Press, Oxford, 1969). Numbers refer to pages.

CLG   *Cours de linguistique générale*. Numbers refer to the pagination of the standard 1922 edition, reproduced in T. de Mauro's *Edition critique* (Payot, Paris, 1972) and in the English translation by R. Harris (Duckworth, London, 1983).

PG   *Philosophical Grammar*, R. Rhees (ed.), A. Kenny (trans.), (Oxford University Press, Oxford, 1974). Numbers refer to pages.

PU   *Philosophische Untersuchungen*, 2nd edn, G. E. M. Anscombe and R. Rhees (eds), G. E. M. Anscombe (trans.) (Oxford University Press, Oxford, 1958). Numbers refer to paragraphs, except when preceded by 'p' (page).

RFM   *Remarks on the Foundations of Mathematics*, 3rd edn, G. H. von Wright, R. Rhees and G. E. M. Anscombe (eds), G. E. M. Anscombe (trans.) (Oxford University Press, Oxford, 1978). Numbers refer to pages.

TLP   *Tractatus Logico-Philosophicus*, corrected 2nd edn, D. F. Pears and B. F. McGuinness (eds and trans.) (Routledge & Kegan Paul, London, 1972). Numbers refer to paragraphs.

1

Texts and Contexts

Saussure owed no intellectual debts to Wittgenstein, and Wittgenstein owed none to Saussure. That, at least, is the assumption from which any comparison between the two must start. They followed academic paths which, as a glance at the relevant biographical facts (see Appendix) shows, might conceivably have crossed during the early years of the present century, but never did. While Saussure was giving his influential lectures on linguistics in Geneva, the young Wittgenstein was studying engineering in Manchester. By the time Wittgenstein wrote the *Tractatus Logico-Philosophicus* Saussure was already dead. Although some people in Wittgenstein's circle of acquaintance (C. K. Ogden, for example) were undoubtedly familiar with Saussure's *Cours de linguistique générale*, there is no indication that Wittgenstein had ever read it. If he had, he never referred to it in his writings, and those who knew Wittgenstein do not recall discussing Saussure with him. On the available evidence, therefore, the mutual independence of Saussure's and Wittgenstein's thinking about language appears to be beyond dispute.

Although these two distinguished academic paths at no point crossed, their twists and turns show a number of configurational likenesses. Both men came from affluent, talented families. Both made their mark with an early work of outstanding brilliance which ruffled scholastic feathers. Wittgenstein's *Tractatus* appeared in the *Annalen der Natürphilosophie* when its author was 32, while Saussure published his *Mémoire sur le système primitif des voyelles dans les langues indo-européennes* when he was only 21. Each, however, owes his ultimate reputation as a major figure to a late work, published posthumously: the *Cours* in Saussure's case and the *Philosophische Untersuchungen* in Wittgenstein's. In both cases, too, the relationship between the earlier and later work is a matter of some controversy.

According to one interpretation, Saussure and Wittgenstein can both be seen as executing a complete volte-face in the course of their academic lives, each of them beginning with one view of language and ending up by rejecting it in favour of a totally different view. According to another interpretation, on the contrary, the alleged differences between the early Saussure and the late Saussure, like those between the early Wittgenstein and the late Wittgenstein, have been much exaggerated. Some critics, therefore, see the work of each thinker as being essentially continuous, while others detect not merely a discontinuity but an outright rejection of positions earlier held.

There is general agreement, however, on the revolutionary impact of the mature work of both in their respective disciplines. Georg von Wright wrote of the later Wittgenstein that he had 'no ancestor in the history of thought. His work signalizes a radical departure from previously existing paths of philosophy' (Fann 1967:23). *Mutatis mutandis,* much the same could be said of the later Saussure and linguistics. In their maturity both Saussure and Wittgenstein were united in viewing language as holding the key to our understanding of the world about us. Moreover, each was deeply concerned with the problem of how, given this pivotal role of language, it was to be possible to establish the academic foundations of his own subject.

In order to appreciate the extent of this concern it is important to situate the work of Saussure and Wittgenstein in the common historical context provided by ideas about language which were current in the universities of nineteenth-century Europe.

* * *

Nineteenth-century Western philosophy was still committed to a view of language which had gone virtually unchallenged for centuries. According to this view, thought and language were separate activities: language was an activity with words and thought was an activity with ideas: words depended on ideas, but ideas did not depend on words. Ideas were treated as standing for objects, properties and relations in the external world, as perceived by the senses. In the mind, these ideas could be combined into propositions, either affirmatively or negatively.

2

Thus in the proposition 'John is dishonest', the separate ideas of 'John' and 'dishonesty' are combined in the mind in a certain way and a certain relationship between them conceived as obtaining. The same relationship is denied in 'John is not dishonest'. These mental operations, it was assumed, could be carried out without having to put the ideas into words. Similarly, it was possible to reason non-verbally. Thus the inference from 'John is dishonest' to 'John should not be placed in a position of trust' was envisaged as a mental transition from one judgement to another judgement, again without any necessary verbal intermediation.

Language enters this picture only when one human being wishes to communicate thoughts to another human being. Thus if I wish to communicate to someone else my judgement that John is dishonest, I can do so by uttering the words 'John is dishonest'; but, so it is assumed, I could also express the same judgement in various other languages, depending on whether I happen to be speaking to an English person, a French person, a German, and so on. So the judgement is not linked to one particular form of words. Any language will do, provided that the language chosen has words for the ideas I wish to communicate, and furthermore has grammatical equipment which allows an appropriate combination of the atomic elements, the separate words. These in turn are associated with the relevant ideas by a purely conventional and historically accidental relationship, differing from one country to another. The theory of the sentence, in short, is that a sentence encodes a judgement, and can be decoded by anybody who happens to be acquainted with the relevant code, i.e. the language. Or at least, this is the philosophically ideal mechanism. According to philosophers, however, this ideal mechanism was not in practice always available, so it was necessary to exercise considerable caution in assuming that the words used were a faithful reflection of the corresponding thoughts or mental operations.

This unreliability, indeed, was one of the prime reasons for language being a subject of philosophical interest at all. Scepticism about the reliability of language goes back in the philosophical tradition at least as far as Bacon (Harris 1981:1ff.). However, it is important here to distinguish between the two ways in which, according to the philosophical tradition, language may mislead. On the one hand, there may be a failure in correspondence between word and reality: the most obvious example of this will be a case in which we have a word for something which simply does not exist, even though it is erroneously believed to exist. For instance, to believe that there is such a substance as phlogiston simply because there is an English word *phlogiston* which purports to be the name of a substance is to be misled in one way by language. In such cases there is no mismatch between the word and the idea: the mismatch is between the idea and the reality. Similarly, in the days when it was believed that the earth was flat, a dictionary definition of the word *earth* which defined it as meaning 'the flat terrestrial body inhabited by the human race' would have been wrong not because the definition failed to correspond to people's idea of the earth, but because it failed to correspond to the geological facts.

Those cases are to be distinguished from a rather different category of linguistic mismatches, where what is misleading is not the idea but the way it is linguistically represented: in other words, what is at fault is the grammar of the expression. A celebrated example of this kind is cited in the Port Royal grammar of 1660. It concerns the use of the definite article. According to the Port Royal grammar, the definite article can be used only in cases where the noun designates something of which there may be many particular examples: for instance, *the house* (there being many houses) or *the man* (there being many men). Therefore it is improper to use the definite article with a proper name, because what a proper name designates is unique. That, allegedly, is why we say, for instance, 'Shakespeare wrote *Hamlet*' and not 'The Shakespeare wrote the *Hamlet*', *Shakespeare* being the proper name of the author and *Hamlet* being the proper name of his play. In Italian, however, common usage does employ the definite article with certain proper names of well-known individuals: for example, *Dante*. This, according to the Port Royal grammarians, is not because Italians have the erroneous idea that there were several authors of the *Divina Commedia*, all of whom happened to be called *Dante*: but simply because Italian usage, for some idiosyncratic reason, fails to employ the definite article correctly in this instance. So the mismatch here is not between the idea and the reality, but rather between the idea and its linguistic expression. It may be useful to distinguish these two types of case by calling the former 'factual misrepresentations' and the latter 'conceptual misrepresentations'. Using this terminology, we may say that when French grammar assigns the masculine gender to the word *professeur*, a double misrepresentation may be involved. If

4

masculine gender is taken to imply male sex, then French grammar here incorporates a factual misrepresentation, in so far as many individuals who may be referred to as *le professeur* are in fact women. But in addition there is a conceptual misrepresentation, in so far as French speakers do not believe that in order to be a teacher you have to be a man. Their idea of a teacher is not one which excludes the possibility of female teachers.

For the nineteenth century, therefore, there was, as it were, a double gap between language and truth. One gap was the potential non-correspondence between linguistic expression and the idea expressed. The other gap was between the idea itself and the facts of the matter.

On these and related questions, nineteenth-century philosophy had the full backing of nineteenth-century philology. Nineteenth-century philology was based on the view that most linguistic facts were merely accidental by-products of cultural evolution. The Comparative Philologists of Germany and France believed that languages were to a large extent at the mercy of the unpredictable hazards of phonetic change. In support of this view, they could cite a large body of empirical evidence: in particular, the evidence of etymology. Thus, for instance, they could point out that the reason why the English word *race* means on the one hand 'competition' and on the other hand 'people, nation' has nothing to do with any connection between the two ideas, but is the chance result of a phonetic convergence between the Old Norse word *ras* and the quite different Old French word *race*. Phenomena of this kind, known technically as 'homonymy', seemed to demonstrate quite clearly that linguistic expression follows its own paths of development, which have nothing to do with the operations of the mind. Consequently, it was impossible to expect any direct correspondence between language and thought.

What convinced the Comparative Philologists of this was the discovery that it was possible to state relationships between the forms of, for example, Sanskrit and Latin, or Latin and French, by reference to purely phonetic laws. In other words, it apparently made no difference what a word meant, or what a construction meant: the development and survival of linguistic forms depended on factors quite unrelated to their meaning. That was the only hypothesis on which Comparative Philology could explain how languages as diverse and mutually incomprehensible as English, Latin, Greek and Sanskrit could, over the space of a relatively short span of human history, have evolved from the same common ancestral language. To take a classic example, it is possible to show that whenever a Latin word begins with the consonant *k* (written *c* in Classical Latin) followed by the vowel *a* (as in the words *canis* 'dog', *carus* 'dear') the derived French words begin with a sibilant (written *ch* in Modern French: *chien* 'dog', *cher* 'dear'). The fact that the words in question have quite separate meanings ('dog' vs. 'dear') evidently has not prevented them from undergoing exactly the same series of phonetic changes. The great achievement of nineteenth-century philology was to demonstrate not merely that this kind of thing actually occurred in recorded time in one civilisation, but that it appeared to be going on constantly, by means of the same or similar processes, in all civilisations at all times. Why it happened, no one could explain: but *that* it happened, and happened regularly, did not seem open to question.

Consequently, in the nineteenth century we find what one might describe as an intellectual consensus between philosophy and philology on the question of the relationship between language and thought. Both agreed in recognising a double disjunction between reality and linguistic expression: one gap between words and ideas, and another gap between ideas and facts. This double disjunction, however, posed acute problems for both disciplines. For philosophy, the problem was this. If human language was an *intrinsically* unreliable guide to the truth, how was it possible to have any confidence in the rational discussion which philosophy itself purported to be? In other words, for the philosopher the problem of language led straight to a problem about the nature and status of philosophy. For the linguist, the problem was different but parallel. If language had no direct connection with reality, but only an arbitrary and ever-changing one, how was it possible to establish linguistics as a scientific form of inquiry? In other words, how was it possible to *explain* linguistic phenomena, as distinct from merely noting and recording their existence? These were the twin problems which Saussure and Wittgenstein inherited. Both made a profound impression upon twentieth-century thought by the originality of the answers they gave.

2

Names and Nomenclatures

Perhaps the most obvious connection between Saussure and Wittgenstein is their common concern to expose certain misconceptions about language. The most important of these shared targets to attack is the view that words function essentially as names of objects or properties already given in advance of language. A striking parallel between the *Cours* and the *Philosophische Untersuchungen* is that in both works the author's main thesis is introduced by way of arguments which may be described as 'anti-nomenclaturist'.

Nomenclaturism has a long history in the Western linguistic tradition. Its oldest and most prestigious form is that in which it appears in Chapter II of the Book of Genesis, where the origin of language is described in the following terms:

> And out of the ground the Lord God formed every beast of the field, and every fowl of the air; and brought them unto Adam to see what he would call them: and whatsoever Adam called every living creature, that was the name thereof.
>
> And Adam gave names to all cattle, and to the fowl of the air, and to every beast of the field.

It would be difficult to exaggerate the influence of these two verses of Genesis on the history of Western linguistics. The development of modern linguistics grew in part out of the dissatisfaction felt by philosophers of the Enlightenment concerning the Biblical account of the origin of language and its subsequent interpretations (Aarsleff 1982). The term *Adamic* emerges as describing a thesis, widely held in the eighteenth century and

7

earlier, which assumes that originally in the Garden of Eden things were called by their correct names, which reflected their true essences; and that the recovery of this 'lost knowledge' is the Holy Grail of linguistic enquiry.

This quasi-mystical approach to language proved extraordinarily tenacious, in part because a number of Enlightenment philosophers were themselves committed to the view that language is a divine gift (Juliard 1970). If one accepts that language is a divine gift, it may well seem to follow that the path to wisdom is to understand the nature of this gift and not to abuse it. This is still the underlying thesis of R. C. Trench's book *On the Study of Words*, published in 1851. Its significance is that Trench, as a prominent Anglican divine, became in the Victorian era one of the most powerful figures in the campaign which led to the publication of the *Oxford English Dictionary*. Trench had no doubt that the English language, properly understood, contains a God-given message; and the title of the original lecture from which his book came was: 'On language as an instrument of knowledge'. No one who reads Trench can imagine for a moment that the battle over the nature of scientific knowledge, which many people suppose had been fought and won in England with the founding of the Royal Society in the seventeenth century, was not still very much alive and in the balance when Queen Victoria at last gave her official approval to the *Oxford English Dictionary*, less than a hundred years ago. In one sense, the whole debate about human knowledge in the Western tradition has always revolved round the relationship between words and the world, between language and reality. This is why the nomenclaturist thesis was central to any number of issues both in linguistics and in philosophy, and continues to be.

It would be a mistake, however, to suppose that Western nomenclaturism is primarily the product of accepting the authority of one particularly prestigious religious text. For it also occurs at a remarkably early date in another strand of the Western tradition which originally owes nothing to Biblical authority. This is the philosophical tradition which goes back to ancient Greece and Plato. Already in the fourth century BC, in Plato's dialogue *Cratylus*, we find the belief that language is not of human origin, coupled with the belief that to understand language is to understand how a name is related to the bearer of that name.

In *Cratylus* the mythical inventor of language is called simply 'the name-maker'. How he originally came to invent language we are never told, but it is assumed that he did not simply coin words at random. On the contrary, he is assumed to have followed certain basic principles of appropriateness in assigning names to things. But in the course of human history, usage has exercised a corrupting influence on language, and these original principles are no longer observed. Hence arises the question with which the dialogue is principally concerned: the question of the 'correctness of names'. From the outset it is clear that this is a controversial issue. In the dialogue, one of the participants, Cratylus, champions a position which we may call 'natural nomenclaturism'. He holds that:

> everything has a right name of its own, which comes by nature, and that a name is not whatever people call a thing by agreement, just a piece of their own voice applied to the thing, but that there is a kind of inherent correctness in names, which is the same for all men, both Greeks and barbarians. (*Cratylus* 383, A/B)

No such doctrine is overtly expressed in the Biblical account. The writer of Genesis does not discuss the question of whether or not Adam named the animals 'correctly', or on what principles he allocated them names; but it was in later times often assumed that Adam's original names were undoubtedly the 'correct' names, in the sense of corresponding appropriately to the nature of the creature in question. Thus Adam was retrospectively cast in the role of the first natural nomenclaturist. This assumption, for example, was the basis of Böhme's belief in a primitive *Natur-Sprache* (Aarsleff 1982:87ff.).

In Plato's dialogue, natural nomenclaturism stands opposed to the view that names are simply arbitrary vocal labels devised to suit human convenience. This is the position taken by Hermogenes, Cratylus' opponent, who claims that 'whatever name you give to a thing is its right name'. For Hermogenes, deciding on a name requires no special expertise of the kind attributed to the mythical name-giver; and no enquiry into the nature of the thing or person named: one name is as good as another. Thus the conflict is presented by Plato as being one between a theory of natural names and a theory of arbitrary names. Although no such conflict emerges in Genesis, the Biblical account appears to agree with Plato's in at least the following particulars. First, names are treated as vocables standing in a certain relationship to the things (persons, etc.) of which they are names. Second, the things thus named are independently given; that is, they exist independently of their being named at all, and independently of what particular name they are assigned.

These two assumptions were never at issue as between natural nomenclaturists and their opponents, either in Graeco-Roman times or later. Locke, for example, maintained that words 'signify only men's peculiar ideas, and that by a perfectly arbitrary imposition' (1706:3.2.8), but accepted that the 'peculiar ideas' were in turn derived from pre-existing things apprehended by the senses. This is crucial to the Lockean distinction between *nominal essences* and *real essences*. Thus for Locke

> the nominal essence of gold is that complex idea the word gold stands for, let it be, for instance, a body yellow, of a certain weight, malleable, fusible and fixed. But the real essence is the constitution of the insensible parts of that body, on which those qualities and all the other properties of gold depend. (1706:3.6.2.)

Leibniz, who rejected Locke's view of arbitrary names, did so in favour of the thesis that there is 'something natural in the origin of words that indicates a relation between things and the sounds and movements of the vocal organs', and so returns, as Aarsleff observes, to a 'modified form of the Platonic doctrine of the nature of language' (Aarsleff 1982:88). But neither Locke nor Leibniz calls in question the notion that what is at issue is how, to put it in terms of Locke's example, the word *gold* relates to gold; or that the nature of gold is in any case independent of the word.

In short, Locke and Leibniz, no less than Cratylus and Hermogenes, espouse an essentially surrogationalist view of language. Surrogationalism accepts as axiomatic the principle that words have meaning for us because words 'stand for' — are surrogates for — something else. Hence the key question is always 'How does this word relate to what it stands for?' This question in turn divides into two parts, or two further questions. One is 'Does this relationship depend on a natural connection of some kind?' (This is the issue which surfaces in the twentieth century as the Saussurean principle of the arbitrariness of the linguistic sign.) The other question is: 'What is it that the word stands for?' (In particular, does it stand for something independently existing in the world; or does it stand simply for an idea in the mind?) Different answers to these further questions distinguish different versions of surrogationalism.

*   *   *

This is the historical background against which the arguments advanced by Saussure and Wittgenstein have to be seen. Although the *Cours* and the *Philosophische Untersuchungen* are both anti-surrogationalist, the versions of surrogationalism they attack are different.

Wittgenstein opens the *Philosophische Untersuchungen* by quoting the passage from St Augustine which gives Augustine's account of how, as a child, he first grasped the significance of speech:

> When they (my elders) named some object, and accordingly moved towards something, I saw this and I grasped that the thing was called by the sound they uttered when they meant to point it out. Their intention was shown by their bodily movements, as it were the natural language of all peoples: the expression of the face, the play of the eyes, the movement of other parts of the body, and the tone of the voice, which expresses our state of mind in seeking, having, rejecting or avoiding something. Thus, as I heard words repeatedly used in their proper places in various sentences, I gradually learnt to understand what objects they signified; and after I had trained my mouth to form these signs, I used them to express my own desires. (*Confessions*,I.8)

Wittgenstein comments on this account as follows:

> These words, it seems to me, give us a particular picture of the essence of human language. It is this: the individual words in language name objects — sentences are combinations of such names. — In this picture of language we find the roots of the following idea: Every word has a meaning. The meaning is correlated with the word. It is the object for which the words stands. (PU:1)

We may compare this with the opening paragraphs of the chapter of the *Cours* devoted to the 'Nature of the Linguistic Sign': 'For some people a language, reduced to its essentials, is a nomenclature: a list of terms corresponding to a list of things. For example, Latin would be represented as follows:' (CLG:97f.). The reader is then presented with a 'picture dictionary' tabulation in two columns. The left-hand column contains a picture of a tree and a picture of a horse. The right-hand column contains the words ARBOR and EQUOS opposite the tree and the horse respectively. Saussure comments:

> This conception is open to a number of objections. It assumes that ideas already exist independently of words. It does not clarify whether the name is a vocal or a psychological entity, for ARBOR might stand for either. Furthermore it leads one to assume that the link between a name and a thing is quite unproblematic, which is far from being the case. None the less, this naive view contains one element of truth, which is that linguistic units are dual in nature, comprising two elements.

The *Cours* then proceeds to set out Saussure's view of the linguistic sign, in opposition to the nomenclaturist picture.

> A linguistic sign is not a link between a thing and a name, but between a concept and a sound pattern. The sound pattern is not actually a sound; for a sound is something physical. A sound pattern is the hearer's psychological impression of a sound, as given to him by the evidence of his senses. This sound pattern may be called a 'material' element only in that it is the representation of our sensory impressions. The sound pattern may thus be distinguished from the other element associated with it in a linguistic sign. This other element is generally of a more abstract kind: the concept. (CLG:98)

So according to Saussure a linguistic sign, as far as the individual language-user is concerned, is a mental association between a concept and a sound pattern. But this is by no means the whole story. For, as Saussure insists repeatedly throughout the *Cours*, one cannot explain the linguistic sign as a mere fact of individual psychology. Every individual, *qua* language-user, is a social being, and language is above all a social phenomenon. The nomenclaturist picture is thus doubly defective. By its crude treatment of words as names of things, it not only fails to represent correctly the reality of language from the individual's point of view, but abstracts from the social dimension altogether.

It is certainly interesting that both Saussure and Wittgenstein choose to introduce their own views of language as views which are, or purport to be, entirely antithetical to the nomenclaturist position. It is all the more interesting in that neither was drawing on any earlier anti-nomenclaturist tradition. Furthermore there is the puzzle in Wittgenstein's case that Augustine's remarks about how he remembered learning language as a child do not come from his philosophical works, but from his autobiography. Furthermore, 'it is not evidently a view any philosopher has adhered to' (Baker and Hacker 1980:xvi). So it seems that Wittgenstein is using Augustine as a convenient whipping boy; and recent commentators (Baker and Hacker 1980:1–27) identify the real philosophical theses which are hidden in this rather naïve Augustinian picture of language as follows.

In attacking the Augustinian picture of language, Wittgenstein is really attacking his own earlier views, those put forward in the *Tractatus*, and at the same time the closely similar views held by other philosophers, notably Russell and Frege. According to the *Tractatus*, 'a name means an object. The object is its meaning [*Bedeutung*]' (TLP:3.203). Furthermore, 'an elementary proposition consists of names. It is a nexus, a concatenation of names . . . It consists of names in immediate combination' (TLP:4.22f.). So the very possibility of propositions (or sentences) is based on the assumption that words stand for things. Hence the *Tractatus* maintains that, in spite of appearances, every possible language must in fact conform to the Augustinian picture. Every proposition really consists of names and is a description of a possible fact. This thesis is closely related to the idea that the basic mechanism of language-learning is ostensive definition: we understand what words mean by having the objects they stand for pointed out to us.

Russell had developed the idea that words are names by positing that they stand not only for concrete things but for abstract things as well. For example, in the sentence *I am in my room*, not only does the word *room* stand for the room, and the word *my* for me, but also the word *in* stands for the relation that holds between me and the room. So the Augustinian picture, as developed by Russell, is not restricted to having physical objects as the meanings of names. This is likewise true for Frege. What Frege counts as 'objects' include numbers, classes, directions of lines, and truth-values. So Wittgenstein's point in picking on Augustine as his target is that Augustine gives us the original, naïve, simple-minded form of the view which philosophers, including Wittgenstein himself, had tried to stretch, adapt and extend to cover as many types of word and meaning as possible.

Now the trouble with this enterprise is that it is totally misguided. The connection between the name *Julius Caesar* and the Roman statesman so named is not at all like the connection between the colour red and the word *red*, and even less like the connection between the word *five* and the number five. What Wittgenstein is attacking, in short, in the nomenclaturist model is the notion that one type of relationship, the name relationship, provides the semantic basis for the whole of language. Augustine, in fact, never goes as far as saying that; nevertheless, his account of his childhood language acquisition provides what has been called a 'proto-theory' (Baker and Hacker 1980:13) and it is this proto-theory which underlies the philosophy of language we find in Frege, Russell and the *Tractatus*.

The case with Saussure is somewhat different, but analogous. Saussure's target is less easily identified, and his objections are not Wittgenstein's. Discussing the nomenclaturist account of the word *arbor*, the *Cours* at least concedes that 'this naive view contains one element of truth, which is that linguistic units are dual in nature, comprising two elements.' (CLG:97–8) This concession brings into sharp relief the difference between Saussure's line of attack and Wittgenstein's. The unidentified nomenclaturists whom Saussure here criticises have at least got one thing right: namely the bi-planar character of the linguistic sign. But this, precisely, is what the Wittgenstein of the *Philosophische Untersuchungen* treats as utterly mistaken. In short, whereas Wittgenstein rejects surrogationalism *in toto*, Saussure rejects only one version of it. Saussure mounts no criticism of those who hold that the word *arbor* 'stands for' a certain concept *unless* they further hold that this concept somehow exists independently of the word *arbor*.

Who are these unidentified nomenclaturists castigated in the *Cours*? Almost certainly not those whom Wittgenstein had in mind. (There is no evidence that Saussure was acquainted with the work of either Russell or Frege.) It is even doubtful whether the nomenclaturism he saw as inimical to the establishment of a true science of language was a linguistic doctrine explicitly formulated as such by its proponents. Rather, what Saussure wished to expose and undermine was the tacit nomenclaturism of a whole tradition of philological investigation which had become established in the universities of nineteenth-century Europe. The Comparative Philologists had assumed that languages were independently comparable from either of two points of view. As Henry Sweet wrote in 1900:

> every sentence or word by which we express our ideas has a certain definite form of its own by virtue of the sounds of which it is made up, and has a more or less definite meaning.
>
> The first thing in the study of language is to realize clearly this duality of form and meaning, constituting respectively the *formal* and the *logical* (or psychological) side of language . . .
>
> The study of the formal side of language is based on *phonetics* — the science of speech sounds; the study of the logical side of language is based on *psychology* — the science of mind. (Sweet 1900:1)

Building on the work of the Comparative Philologists, the Neogrammarians had sought to establish the existence of historical sound laws, operating irrespective of the meanings of words; their success in this endeavour reinforced the view that what Sweet calls the 'formal' side of language and the 'logical' side of language could be studied quite separately. This theoretical divorce between form and meaning was further bolstered by the discredit into which natural nomenclaturism had fallen, and the general acceptance of the thesis that, with a few minor and unimportant exceptions, the relation between form and meaning in language was entirely arbitrary. The consensus view of nineteenth-century linguists was, as W. D. Whitney wrote in 1875, that 'The tie existing between the conception and the sign is one of mental association only, a mental association as artificial as connects, for example, the sign 5 with the number it stands for, or π with 3.14159+' (Whitney 1875:115).

Hence it seemed unquestionable to most linguists of Saussure's generation that it was perfectly legitimate — indeed essential — to distinguish two orders of question concerning linguistic phenomena. One could start with forms and enquire into their meanings; or one could start from meanings and enquire how they were formally expressed. Sweet provided the following example from the investigation of grammar:

in the scientific investigation of a language we can either take such a form as the nominative case — supposing the language has one — and examine its syntactical uses or grammatical meaning; or we can take such a grammatical relation as that of subject and predicate, and inquire into the different ways in which it is expressed grammatically either in some language or group of languages or in language in general. (Sweet 1900:7–8)

This example probably illustrates as clearly as any the view Saussure rejects. Saussure rightly sees this position as assuming the validity of a nomenclaturist approach to language. It presupposes that we can *first* define what the nominative case is, or the nominative case form, and *then* look to see whether or how any given language expresses it. This is exactly the methodological assumption on which the whole of nineteenth-century Comparative Philology was based. But Saussure saw it as embodying a fundamental error: for the grammatical phenomenon (or range of grammatical phenomena) we call 'the nominative case' is language-relative. It is neither itself a linguistic universal nor a set of language-neutral criteria which are somehow guaranteed to be universally applicable. Thus, for Saussure, it *makes no sense* to ask questions such as 'Does the nominative case survive from Latin into French?' or even 'How many languages of the world have a nominative case?' And, *mutatis mutandis*, the same goes for questions like 'Does the Latin word *arbor* survive into French?' and 'How many languages of the world have a word for "tree"?' But these are the kinds of question on which the nineteenth century had sought to lay the foundations of linguistics.

In attacking nomenclaturism Saussure, like Wittgenstein, was attacking a view of language he had formerly held (although, unlike Wittgenstein, had never propounded in the form of a book). Throughout the whole of his career he had taught a syllabus of Indo-European studies based essentially upon the 'picture dictionary' model of the relationship between words and meanings. Linguistic evolution, on this view, was a process in which the 'tree' remained constant over time, while different phonetic forms (*arbor, arbre,* etc.) successively became attached to it at different times and in different places.

* * *

The anti-nomenclaturism of the *Cours* and the *Philosophische Untersuchungen* is thus directed towards very different ends. Both works concur, however, in diagnosing as a major source of trouble the traditional thesis that the meaning of a word is 'the object for which the word stands'. Both further concur, at least in certain respects, in their analysis of the nomenclaturist error. Language is not, as the nomenclaturist implies, a set of relations between independently given sounds or marks on the one hand and independently given features of the external world on the other. To view language thus is both to isolate words from the linguistic systems to which they belong and, simultaneously, to isolate the language-user from the linguistic community.

3

Linguistic Units

Any theorist of language who starts by rejecting nomenclaturism is immediately left with two theoretical gaps to fill. If a word is not a vocable standing for an object, what is it? If the meaning of a word is not to be construed on the model of the naming relation, how is it to be construed? As Saussure and Wittgenstein both saw, these two questions are in fact different facets of one and the same problem: the problem of the identity of linguistic units.

It appears to be a matter of common sense that the linguistic units of the kind we ordinarily call 'words', 'phrases' and 'sentences' somehow must have determinate identities. For if we could not recognise them, combine them and thus use them for purposes of communication, it seems that we could never master language at all. Language, indeed, would be unthinkable unless it were possible for people to identify without difficulty instances of saying the same thing, repeating the same words, asking the same questions, and so on (and, *pari passu*, instances of not saying the same thing, not repeating the same words, asking a different question). In brief, the very essence of language seems to depend on the possibility of regular recurrence of verbal items of various kinds. The theoretical problem is to explain what guarantees this possibility. Any general analysis of how language works is thus forced to tackle the notion of linguistic units.

'The mechanism of a language,' says Saussure, 'turns entirely on identities and differences. The latter are merely counterparts of the former' (CLG:151). The beginning of linguistic wisdom, for Saussure, is to see that the nomenclaturist has no satisfactory account of the identity of linguistic units, and hence no viable theory of language. For Wittgenstein, this conclusion emerges

19

even if we restrict attention to communication systems which *prima facie* lend themselves to analysis along nomenclaturist lines. At the beginning of the *Philosophische Untersuchungen* he describes a primitive language of this kind.

> The language is meant to serve for communication between a builder A and an assistant B. A is building with building-stones: there are blocks, pillars, slabs and beams. B has to pass the stones, and that in the order in which A needs them. For this purpose they use a language consisting of the words "block", "pillar", "slab", "beam". A calls them out; B brings the stone which he has learnt to bring at such-and-such a call. — Conceive this as a complete primitive language. (PU:2)

The nomenclaturist will insist on pinning down the identity of the linguistic units to the correlations obtaining between certain types of call ('Block', 'Pillar', etc.) and certain types of building stone (blocks, pillars, etc.). But this will not do, for a very simple reason. It avails nothing to tell us that here we have four different words 'standing for' four different types of building stone. The correlation between 'Block' and blocks, 'Pillar' and pillars, etc. is a correlation imposed by the communication system, not a result of some independent connection between the sounds and the objects. In short, the nomenclaturist has mistaken an explanandum for an explanation.

Reduced to its most basic terms, the problem of linguistic identity for both Saussure and Wittgenstein is a generalisation of the question: what distinguishes occurrences of the same linguistic sign from occurrences of different linguistic signs? There is doubtless a temptation to reply that in one case the meanings will be the same, whereas in the other case the meanings will be different. But, as both writers are at pains to make clear, such a summary reply merely parries the question. Wittgenstein makes this point, significantly, with reference to the 'verb of identity' itself: the verb *to be*.

> What does it mean to say that the "is" in "The rose is red" has a different meaning from the "is" in "twice two is four"? If it is answered that it means that different rules are valid for these two words, we can say we have only *one* word here. — And if all I am attending to is grammatical rules, these

do allow the use of the word "is" in both connexions. (PU:558)

Saussure goes further, pointing out that the identity of a linguistic sign by no means requires identical realisations on every occasion of its use.

> For example, we may hear in the course of a lecture several repetitions of the word *Messieurs!* ('Gentlemen!'). We feel that in each case it is the same expression: and yet there are variations of delivery and intonation which give rise in the several instances to very noticeable phonic differences — differences as marked as those which in other cases serve to differentiate one word from another . . . Furthermore, this feeling of identity persists in spite of the fact that from a semantic point of view too there is no absolute reduplication from one *Messieurs!* to the next. A word can express quite different ideas without seriously compromising its own identity. (CLG:150–1)

But a French native speaker will have no difficulty in telling us how many times the word *messieurs* occurred in the speech, in spite of the phonetic and semantic variations which characterised its various occurrences. Similarly, to cite another example Saussure gives, there will be no hesitation in recognising that the expressions *adopter une mode* ('to adopt a fashion') and *adopter un enfant* ('to adopt a child') exemplify uses of the same French verb, even though the 'adoption' involved is entirely different in the two cases (CLG:151). Such examples demonstrate, for Saussure, the futility of any attempt to construe the identity of a linguistic sign in terms of the invariance of its phonetic or semantic manifestations on different occasions. What kind of 'sameness', then, is the sameness we appeal to in claiming that the speaker uttered 'the same word' several times in the course of his speech? To answer this question, clearly, is at the same time to specify what it is that constitutes the identity of the word (e.g. of the French word *messieurs*). It is noteworthy that neither Saussure nor Wittgenstein entertains for a moment the possibility that linguistic identity is illusory, or that it constitutes some kind of special case. On the contrary, for Wittgenstein 'saying the same thing' is clearly just one example of 'doing the same thing': analogous general criteria will apply. Wittgenstein asks:

Suppose someone gets the series of numbers, 1, 3, 5, 7, .. by working out the series $2x + 1$. And now he asks himself: "But am I always doing the same thing, or something different every time?"

If from one day to the next you promise "To-morrow I will come and see you" — are you saying the same thing every day, or every day something different? (PU:226)

Wittgenstein, like Saussure, never lets us forget that what counts as 'the same' and what counts as 'different' will depend on the point of view taken. If the point of view changes, then the answer to the question 'Is it the same?' may also change. But both take it for granted that if we wish to understand how language works, then we must grant the validity of at least one point of view from which it makes sense to envisage a determinate identification of linguistic items. The very question as to whether saying 'Tomorrow I will come and see you' on successive days is saying the same thing or something different would lose its bite were it not presupposed that *that* combination of words can at least be identified as 'the same' from one day to the next. So the sentence *Tomorrow I will come and see you* can be produced in answer both to a question about what you promised yesterday and also to a question about what you promised today. At the very least, it appears, a theorist has to concede that you said the same thing in so far as you used the same English sentence on two successive days, and 'what you said' on both occasions is correctly reported, at least on one level, by reiterating that same English sentence. It is this level of sameness that Saussure is also focussing on with his *Messieurs!* example. For if our account of language cannot even characterise the sameness involved at this level, it can hardly pass muster as a plausible analysis at all.

Furthermore, both Saussure and Wittgenstein appear to be in agreement that this level of sameness has to incorporate linguistic meaning. Neither is interested in any attempt to account for the recognised recurrence of words or sentences by excluding semantic considerations. Both concur (i) that the linguistic meaning of a word is not an extra-linguistic entity of any kind, and (ii) that whatever linguistic meaning a word has depends on a complex network of relations which link it to other words.

Wittgenstein opens the *Blue Book* with the question 'What is the meaning of a word?' The general answer he offers applies not only to words, but to linguistic units of any kind: 'The sign (the sentence) gets its significance from the system of signs, from the language to which it belongs.' (BB:5) More bluntly, in the *Philosophische Grammatik* we are told: 'the use of a word in the language is its meaning' (PG:60).

This is a formula which Saussure would have had no difficulty in endorsing, albeit with caveats about the word *word* (CLG:147ff.). For Saussure, the meaning of any linguistic sign is not isolable from that of other signs in *la langue*. This is because he envisages a language as a system of signs held together by chains of syntagmatic and associative relations. Syntagmatic relations he describes as relations *in praesentia* (CLG:171): in the phrase *my house* the individual signs *my* and *house* are syntagmatically related. Such relations are invariably expressed in the dimension of linearity, even though they are not linear relations as such. Associative relations Saussure describes as relations *in absentia* (CLG:171): in *my house* the individual sign *my* is associatively related to *you*, *his*, *her*, etc., while the sign *house* is associatively related to *home*, *domicile*, *dwelling*, *apartment*, etc. The phrase *my house* thus represents a syntagmatically organised selection from a large range of associatively organised possibilities made available by the language.

Saussure illustrates the interconnection between syntagmatic and associative relations by means of a comparison:

> a linguistic unit may be compared to a single part of a building, e.g. a column. A column is related in a certain way to the architrave it supports. This disposition, involving two units co-present in space, is comparable to a syntagmatic relation. On the other hand, if the column is Doric, it will evoke mental comparison with the other architectural orders (Ionic, Corinthian, etc.), which are not in this instance spatially co-present. This relation is associative. (CLG:171)

Although Wittgenstein draws no explicit distinction between syntagmatic and associative relations, his notion of meaning as 'use in the language' is not as far from Saussure's way of thinking as might at first sight appear. For Saussure, the total meaning of a linguistic sign, its value (*valeur*), is also its use in the language: that is, its potential use in certain syntagmatic combinations (but not others), together with its distinctive use in associative contrast with other signs which might have occurred in those combinations.

* * *

In order to explain what kind of identity linguistic units have both Saussure and Wittgenstein appeal constantly to an analogy with games. The attraction of this analogy for theorists who have begun by rejecting nomenclaturism is evident. In order to explain the workings of a game there is no temptation to look for connections with things extraneous to the game itself. The game is in an important sense *self-contained*, and yet it is not a mere abstraction; nor are its constitutive elements abstractions. Wittgenstein writes:

> We are talking about the spatial and temporal phenomenon of language, not about some non-spatial, non-temporal phantasm . . . But we talk about it as we do about the pieces in chess when we are stating the rules of the game, not describing their physical properties.
> The question "What is a word really?" is analogous to "What is a piece in chess?" (PU:108)

Chess is also Saussure's favourite metaphor (CLG:43, 125–7, 135, 149, 153–4) and early on in the *Cours* he makes a closely related point to Wittgenstein's about the parallel between chessmen and words:

> If pieces made of ivory are substituted for pieces made of wood, the change makes no difference to the system. But if the number of pieces is diminished or increased, that is a change which profoundly affects the 'grammar' of the game. (CLG:43)

One may compare this with Wittgenstein's remark at the beginning of the *Brown Book*:

> Suppose a man described a game of chess, without mentioning the existence and operations of the pawns. His description of the game as a natural phenomenon will be incomplete. On the other hand we may say that he has completely described a simpler game. (BB:77)

Changing the number of pieces changes the game, whereas changing their physical composition or even their shape does not, provided always that any such change does not obliterate the distinctive identities of the different pieces. Saussure invites us to

24

consider what constitutes the identity of a knight in chess:

> Consider a knight in chess. Is the piece by itself an element
> of the game? Certainly not. For as a material object,
> separated from its square on the board and the other
> conditions of play, it is of no significance for the player. It
> becomes a real, concrete element only when it takes on or
> becomes identified with its value in the game. Suppose that
> during a game this piece gets lost or destroyed. Can it be
> replaced? Of course it can. Not only by some other knight,
> but even by an object of quite a different shape, which can
> be counted as a knight, provided it is assigned the same
> value as the missing piece. (CLG:153–4)

For both Saussure and Wittgenstein the fundamental error of
nomenclaturism is rather like supposing that appealing to
something outside the game of chess is necessary in order to
explain the significance and function of the chessmen. Not only
is such an appeal *un*necessary, but it would betray a profound
failure to grasp what chess is. Likewise, the appeal to what lies
'outside' language in order to explain the significance and function
of linguistic elements betrays a profound failure to grasp what
language is.

* * *

The chess comparison would be extremely important in the
work of both Saussure and Wittgenstein even if all it did was to
illuminate what kind of identity a linguistic unit has. But it does
far more than that. It simultaneously throws light on meaning,
on the nature of linguistic rules, and on the relationship between
language and thought. In short, it represents a radical shift of
perspective on language, replacing the nomenclaturist view by
one from which the language user is seen essentially as the player
of a game. For Saussure this is a shift which at one stroke clarifies
the whole enterprise of linguistic description and at last makes it
possible to place the science of linguistics on a sound theoretical
basis. For Wittgenstein, it is the philosopher's antidote to that
'bewitchment of our intelligence by means of language' (PU:109)
which it is the business of philosophy to dispel.

Wittgenstein appears to have borrowed the games analogy from
earlier discussions in the philosophy of mathematics, but he uses

it in a variety of original ways (Baker and Hacker 1980:47ff.). Similarly, Saussure does not limit himself to just one interpretation of the correspondence between language and chess. Nevertheless, there is what Wittgenstein would doubtless have categorised as a 'family resemblance' linking the uses which he and Saussure make of the comparison.

The consequence of adopting this new linguistic perspective is far-reaching in both cases. Its most conspicuous effects will be explored under separate heads in the chapters that follow. Although Saussure and Wittgenstein in the final analysis diverge very fundamentally on some issues in their account of language, even these divergences can illuminatingly be seen as alternative routes branching from a shared point of departure.

4

Language and Thought

The most sweeping revision which accompanies the rejection of a nomenclaturist perspective in favour of a games perspective is a revision of the entire relationship between language and thought. In Wittgenstein's case, the revision is writ large in the development of his own views. In the *Tractatus* he had claimed that 'Language disguises thought. So much so, that from the outward form of the clothing it is impossible to infer the form of thought beneath it. . . ' (TLP:4.002) But by the time he wrote the *Philosophische Grammatik* he held that 'When I think in language, there aren't meanings going through my mind in addition to the verbal expressions; the language is itself the vehicle of thought.' (PG:161). Traditionally, the assumed priority of thought over language is summed up in Aristotle's famous pronouncement:

> Words spoken are symbols or signs of affections or impressions of the soul; written words are the signs of words spoken. As writing, so also is speech not the same for all races of men. But the mental affections themselves, of which these words are primarily signs, are the same for the whole of mankind, as are also the objects of which those affections are representations or likenesses, images, copies. (*De Interpretatione*, I)

According to this Aristotelian view, words come logically and psychologically last in a natural order of progression, which begins with the 'objects' of the real world. If there were no such objects, human beings would have no 'representations' of them in the form of 'mental affections'; and if there were no such mental affections there would in turn be nothing for words to be signs of. For Aristotle, any vocal noise which is not the sign of a mental affection is simply not a word, and hence not part of language. Correspondingly it will always make sense, in Aristotelian terms, to ask what thought a word expresses: and identifying the thought in question becomes a standard way of explaining what the word means.

Within a conceptual framework of the Aristotelian variety it also makes sense, and may be more convenient, to explain the meaning of a word by bypassing the thought and pointing directly to the object, of which the thought is merely a 'representation'. Thus someone who wishes to know what the word *elephant* means can most reliably be acquainted with this information by being shown an elephant: for elephants, according to Aristotle, are 'the same for the whole of mankind', and so are the corresponding mental affections. Indeed, if I have never seen an elephant, but only heard second-hand reports about this animal, a strict Aristotelian might perhaps wish to question whether I really know the meaning of the word *elephant*. (This form of Aristotelian intransigence survives vestigially in the claims of those who maintain that one thing a person born blind cannot do is understand the meaning of the word *red*: or, for that matter, any other colour word.)

A quite different conceptual framework becomes available once the 'games' perspective is adopted. If words are like chess pieces, it makes little sense to ask what thought the word *elephant* expresses; one might as well ask a chess expert what thought the knight expresses, or ask someone to point out a real knight by way of explanation. Rather, in order to understand what a knight 'means' in chess one needs to know its role in the game. To be sure, one can still distinguish between the wooden or ivory knight on the board and a corresponding concept (the concept of a 'chess knight'). But the latter does not explain the former: for they are indivisible counterparts. To ask how the piece moves on the board *is* to ask for an elucidation of the concept 'chess knight'.

It is this indivisibility which motivates the Saussurean doctrine of signal (*signifiant*) and signification (*signifié*). The association between sound pattern and concept which constitutes the linguistic sign is not an association of independently given items. The chapter in the *Cours* on 'Linguistic Value' takes great pains to make this clear. One particularly memorable comparison invokes the recto and verso of a sheet of paper.

28

Just as it is impossible to take a pair of scissors and cut one side of paper without at the same time cutting the other, so it is impossible in a language to separate sound from thought, or thought from sound. To separate the two for theoretical purposes takes us into either pure psychology or pure phonetics, not linguistics. (CLG:157)

Certainly it is possible to describe what is on the phonetic recto separately from describing what is on the conceptual verso; and to do this for any given linguistic sign. But equally it is possible to describe the shape of a knight in chess without describing the configuration of moves it makes. That in no way alters the truth that a chess knight is neither just a piece of a certain shape, nor just a configuration of moves. Someone who had been taught the various configurations of moves made by different chess pieces, but not which pieces make which moves, would no more be able to play chess than someone would be able to speak or understand French who had been taught (if that were possible) just the meaning of French words without being taught which words meant what.

In short, in the perspective adopted by Saussure and Wittgenstein, the function of a word is no longer to be explained by reference to the thought it allegedly expresses; nor the thought in turn to be explained by reference to some 'object' or feature of the external world which it mentally 'represents'. Instead the word, now treated as an indivisible unit of sound-with-sense, is explained by contrasting its role with that of other words in the linguistic system of which it forms part. The upshot of this revaluation is to make thought (or at least those forms of thought which are propositionally articulated and generally held to characterise the human intellect) in all important respects language-related. Thinking is no longer an autonomous, self-sustaining activity of the human mind, and speech merely its externalisation. On the contrary, speech and thought are interdependent, neither occurring without the other, and both made possible by language.

This emphasis on the interdependent relationship between thinking and speaking emerges with different nuances in the work of both thinkers. Saussure roundly denies the possibility of pre-linguistic thought:

Psychologically, setting aside its expression in words, our

thought is simply a vague, shapeless mass . . . No ideas are established in advance, and nothing is distinct, before the introduction of linguistic structure. (CLG:155)

Nor, on the other hand, does sound offer 'a ready-made mould, with shapes that thought must inevitably conform to' (CLG:155). How, then, should we envisage the connection between the phonic and the ideational aspects of language? In one of the most arresting metaphorical images of the *Cours*, Saussure compares the way thought combines with sound to the contact between air and water (CLG:156). What the observer sees as surface ripples are shapes caused by local variations in pressure between the mass of air and the mass of water. However strained or curious the reader may find this comparison, it is at least clear why Saussure invokes it. The intention is evidently to drive home two points. First, we should not think of language as constituting some mysterious third layer which mediates between thought and expression: between air and water there is no intermediate layer, and yet the interface is configurationally articulated. Second, the configurations at the interface are *simultaneously* configurations of *both* the masses in contact, and the indentations match exactly: the fact that we 'see' them as ripples on the water and not as ripples in the air is simply due to the fact that for us the water is 'visible' whereas the air is 'invisible'. Similarly, the sound of a word is perceptible, whereas its meaning is not: but neither has a separate linguistic existence.

Wittgenstein does not indulge in such flights of metaphorical fancy, and he is more circumspect than Saussure on the possibility of thought without language. He appears to hold that even for creatures without language certain simple forms of thought are possible; but that others require a structural complexity which only language affords. 'A dog believes his master is at the door. But can he also believe his master will come the day after tomorrow?' (PU:p.174) Nevertheless, in the same passage, he raises the question 'Can only those hope who can talk?' and gives the answer:

Only those who have mastered the use of a language. That is to say, the phenomena of hope are modes of this complicated form of life. (PU:p.174)

Earlier in the *Philosophische Untersuchungen*, however, we find the observation:

> It is sometimes said that animals do not talk because they
> lack the mental capacity. And this means: "they do not
> think, and that is why they do not talk." But — they simply
> do not talk. Or to put it better: they do not use language
> — if we except the most primitive forms of language. (PU:25)

This qualification, although added almost as an afterthought, is
of some significance. For, like the remark about a dog's beliefs,
it seems to indicate a readiness to concede that language is not
sharply demarcated from non-linguistic behaviour (and hence
that what is possible through language is not sharply demarcated
either).

The mental capacity of animals is not a substantive issue as
far as Wittgenstein is concerned. (He would doubtless have
regarded any experimental programme designed to test whether
or not chimpanzees can master the rudiments of language as
bizarrely misconceived.) Nevertheless, our willingness to attribute
or deny to animals various language-related abilities is of interest
because it is all of a piece with the way we conceptualise our own
abilities. The question is not whether a dog 'really' believes his
master is at the door, but that it makes sense to say so as a
comment on the dog's behaviour; whereas it makes none to say
the dog hopes that this is the case. And this has nothing to do
with whether a dog can bark to himself *sotto voce* the canine sentence
'My master is at the door.' Thinking is not, for Wittgenstein,
some kind of inner monologue. 'Is thinking a kind of speaking?
One would like to say it is what distinguishes speech with thought
from talking without thinking.' (PU:330) But in that respect words
occupy no privileged status linking the internal and external
activities. 'Speech with and without thought is to be compared
with the playing of a piece of music with and without thought.'
(PU:341) Certainly there is such a thing as formulating our
thoughts verbally without giving utterance to them. But that is
no more — and no less — a form of thinking than uttering the
words aloud. Indeed, there would be no way of saying the words
silently unless one could also give them audible utterance.

Wittgenstein cites the evidence produced by William James
concerning the recollections of a deaf mute, who claimed that in
his early youth, before learning to speak, he had had thoughts
about God, and had also, before learning to write, asked himself
questions about the origin of the world. This James took as
showing that thought is possible without language. Wittgenstein

remains unconvinced by the deaf mute's story: 'Are you sure —
one would like to ask — that this is the correct translation of your
wordless thought into words?' (PU:342)

Wittgenstein does not deny that certain behaviour may
appropriately be described in terms of a person having certain
wordless thoughts:

> I might also act in such a way while taking various
> measurements that an onlooker would say I had — without
> words — thought: If two magnitudes are equal to a
> third, they are equal to one another. — But what con-
> stitutes thought here is not some process which has to
> accompany the words if they are not to be spoken without
> thought. (PU:330)

Nor does he deny that we often find ourselves making a mental
effort commonly described as 'searching for the right words' to
express an idea. But it is unclear what this shows about the
psychological process involved. 'Now if it were asked: "Do you
have the thought before finding the expression?" what would one
have to reply? And what, to the question: "What did the thought
consist in, as it existed before its expression?" ' (PU:335)

These become particularly interesting questions if we apply
them to Saussure's account of the process by which thoughts are
put into verbal form through the operations of the 'speech circuit'
(*circuit de la parole*). According to Saussure, this circuit begins in
the brain of the speaker when the occurrence of a certain concept
triggers a corresponding sound pattern, which in turn triggers
motor instructions to the organs of phonation (CLG:28). Such a
model allows us to envisage various possible Saussurean answers
to Wittgenstein's questions.

(a) The search for the right expression corresponds to a case
in which the speaker cannot decide which of various verbal
possibilities best suits the demands of a particular speech situation.
The hesitation is occasioned by the fact that the language affords
a variety of signs or combinations of signs, and there is an
embarrassment of choice. The games analogue here is that of the
player who cannot decide which move to make. Should one
advance the queen or withdraw the knight? Go for the cross-court
pass or the top-spin lob? (In the end, the momentary indecision
may cost you the point.) Various more or less desperate varieties

of this type of case may occur. It may seem that any one of the available possibilities would do at a pinch; but one hesitates nevertheless, in case there were a better option one had not thought of. Or, on the contrary, it may seem that none of the possibilities which occur to one is really satisfactory. (The cross-court pass will be difficult from this angle; but one's opponent is not really close enough in to lob.) But in all these cases the Saussurean answer to Wittgenstein is in principle clear. 'Yes, I had the thought before finding the expression. What did it consist in, as it existed before its expression? It consisted in a speech gap which needed filling, a games problem posed by a particular episode of play.'

(b) A different type of case would be the hesitation caused by a failure to come up with the expression one knows is right but cannot lay one's tongue on. What on earth is that particular shade of green called? What was the name of that flower which used to grow in our garden when we were children? Here again the Saussurean account is reasonably clear. The speaker has identified the *signifié* but has temporarily mislaid the *signifiant*. Somehow the triggering process which normally connects the two has become blocked. Here again it is justifiable to say that one did indeed have the thought before finding the expression. But in this instance what it consisted in, prior to finding its expression, was our unhesitating identification of a particular communicational requirement. (It was *that* colour, or *that* flower.) The games analogue is the rarer case of forgetting how to make the move required: it is a temporary lapse in one's practical command of the rules.

(c) Saussure's model also allows for a third and more interesting type of case: coming up with a novel expression. One may well hesitate before doing so, and search for other possibilities. ('Is that really a word?' 'Can one really say that?') The example Saussure discusses (CLG:227) is the first use of the word *indécorable* ('undecorable'). *Ex hypothesi* the speaker has never heard this word before: the mental 'search' for it is therefore of a different order from the search for a familiar expression which eludes one. What Saussure says about this type of case is that although the word *indécorable* may never have been used before, nevertheless the pattern for its formation already existed. (Many French adjectives combine stem, negative prefix, and suffix *-able*.) Thus the case is not like that of the first schoolboy at Rugby who picked up the ball and ran: for he simply broke the rules. The games analogue for *indécorable* is that of exploiting a combination of possibilities which the rules allow, but which no previous player has ever had the wit — or the need — to use.

The Saussurean account of the above types of case is perfectly consistent with Wittgenstein's position. What Wittgenstein is anxious to establish is that we are mistaken if we think that speech is meaningful in virtue of some hidden thought process which accompanies it, just as we would be mistaken if we thought that a game of chess was meaningful in virtue of something going on in the minds of the players; but rather that what matters is taking place on the chess board. To understand what is taking place there we do not need to be privy to the mental activities of the players; we simply need to understand the game of chess. So it is with speech. Access to what is happening in the heads of the interlocutors is not what is relevant: what is relevant is to know their language. Furthermore, a chess player's 'chess thoughts' are exhibited in the moves made publicly on the board: they are not mysterious inner events which only the player is aware of. In that sense, thinking chess *is* just playing chess. Similarly, according to Wittgenstein, we are liable to misconceive what happens in the case of language.

> We are tempted to think that the action of language consists of two parts; an inorganic part, the handling of the signs, and an organic part, which we may call understanding these signs, meaning them, interpreting them, thinking. These latter activities seem to take place in a queer kind of medium, the mind; and the mechanism of the mind, the nature of which, it seems, we don't quite understand, can bring about effects which no material mechanism could. (BB:3)

But the temptation to accept this division between an 'organic' and an 'inorganic' part of language should be resisted: for 'thinking is essentially the activity of operating with signs. This activity is performed by the hand, when we think by writing; by the mouth and larynx, when we think by speaking.' (BB:6)

Stated in these terms, Wittgenstein's thesis may sound superficially like a brash form of behaviourism, particularly when taken in conjunction with Wittgensteinian coat-trailing *boutades* such as 'If one sees the behaviour of a living thing, one sees its soul' (PU:357). In the *Philosophische Untersuchungen* Wittgenstein deals dismissively with this charge. His imaginary interlocutor at one point says: 'Are you not really a behaviourist in disguise? Aren't you at bottom really saying that everything except human behaviour is a fiction?' (PU:307) Wittgenstein's reply is mockingly epigrammatic: 'If I do speak of a fiction, then it is of a *grammatical* fiction.' (PU:307) The full savour of this reply is lost without an appreciation of the characteristically Wittgensteinian notion of 'grammar' (see Chapter 7). But Wittgenstein might equally well have rebutted the accusation simply by pointing out that it would be rather ridiculous to set up an opposition between a 'behaviourist' and a 'mentalist' theory of chess. For no one seriously supposes that whether or not A and B are playing chess is determined by their mental efforts. It is determined on the one hand by the way they move the pieces on the board, and on the other hand by the rules of the game.

5

Systems and Users

One obvious corollary of accepting the games analogy is that it invites, or rather demands, recognition of a linguistic distinction corresponding to that between a game, together with its constituent parts, considered as an organised type of activity (chess versus tennis versus cricket, etc.) and the pursuit of this activity on particular occasions by particular individuals, their successes or failures, their muscular movements, and so on. Saussure responds to this demand by differentiating explicitly and systematically between *langue* and *parole*. Wittgenstein, on the other hand, introduces no terminological expedient of this kind; nor does he stress the importance of such a distinction with the insistence that we find throughout the *Cours*. He is simply content to point out that signs are not to be confused with the physiological mechanics of their production. Thus when a sentence is uttered

> very complicated processes takes place in the larynx, the speech muscles, the nerves, etc. These are *accompaniments* of the spoken sentence. And the sentence itself remains the only thing that interests us — not as part of a mechanism, but as part of a calculus. (PG:104)

This corresponds exactly to Saussure's position; but Wittgenstein accords the distinction less prominence. The explanation of this difference of emphasis doubtless in part lies in the antecedent histories of linguistics and philosophy respectively.

Although Wittgenstein came to believe that Frege, Russell and his own *Tractatus* had propagated serious misconceptions about language, he did not believe that those misconceptions were primarily due, or even due at all, to a failure to grasp a fundamental distinction between a system and its use. Whereas

Saussure saw this as the most deep-seated and vitiating weakness of nineteenth-century linguistic studies. In his view it was because his predecessors had constantly muddled up *faits de langue* with *faits de parole* that so little progress had been made towards establishing linguistics as a science. For without that foundational distinction it becomes impossible to establish a further dichotomy which Saussure also regarded as indispensable for his science, between synchronic linguistics and diachronic linguistics. The great paradox of nineteenth-century linguistics, for Saussure, was that its concentration of effort on the detailed differences over time which historical comparisons reveal had resulted in a total failure to understand the nature of linguistic change.

The *Cours* gives numerous examples of the mistakes and incoherences which ensue. It becomes impossible to establish whether pronunciations such as *se fâcher* and *se fôcher* are variants of the same linguistic sign or two different linguistic signs (CLG:249). It becomes plausible to misconstrue the appearance of analogical forms such as Latin *honos* as products of linguistic change (CLG:221ff.). It becomes commonplace to formulate synchronic and diachronic generalisations in terms which fail to distinguish between them (CLG:130–1). Worse still, quite spurious 'explanations' are given: 'For instance, the present meaning of the French word *père* is explained by appeal to the fact that its Latin etymon *pater* meant "father" ' (CLG:136).

Saussure held that had linguists realised the importance of distinguishing from the outset, as in the case of games, between facts pertaining to the structure of the game itself, facts pertaining to individual episodes of play, and facts pertaining to the historical evolution of the game, all these confusions could have been avoided, and the correct relationships would have been established between the various types of phenomena with which linguistics is concerned. In particular, linguists would have seen that it is essential to separate 'internal' from 'external' considerations. Saussure draws that distinction again by allusion to chess.

> In the case of chess, it is relatively easy to distinguish between what is external and what is internal. The fact that chess came from Persia to Europe is an external fact, whereas everything which concerns the system and its rules is internal. If pieces made of ivory are substituted for pieces made of wood, the change makes no difference to the system. (CLG:43)

What thus emerges as of prime importance in Saussurean linguistics is to distinguish between 'the system' and everything else. For it is the system which limits the possibilities in particular episodes of play, which determines the significance of each individual move, and which the players have to abide by (if their conduct is not to be open to objection as being 'out of order', i.e. in violation of the rules). The system is by definition synchronic. 'A language is a system of which all the parts can and must be considered as synchronically interdependent.' (CLG:124) More exactly, the system is 'idiosynchronic' (CLG:128); in other words, it does not embrace everything which is historically related and contemporaneous, but only the synchronic interdependences. In this respect, it is exactly analogous to a game. For instance, although real tennis and lawn tennis are historically related, and both survive as contemporary games, it would be absurd to suppose that tennis players might sometimes confuse the two, or that a match could be played which was simultaneously lawn tennis and real tennis, or that the men's final at Wimbledon should be taken as deciding the real tennis championship as well. But none of this in any way precludes the possibility of tracing both games back to a common ancestor.

Some commentators see Saussure's preoccupation with systems as dating back to the publication of the *Mémoire*. Certainly the word *système* already appears in its title. What Saussure tackles in the *Mémoire* is a problem about primitive Indo-European which had long vexed Comparative Philologists. The question was what vowels to postulate for this ancestral language in order to account satisfactorily for the vowels of the attested languages later derived from it; and the troublesome vowel was *a*. Before Saussure, philologists had already established that there must originally have been two different kinds of *a*, because the assumption that there was only one failed to match the evidence from derived languages. Saussure's contribution was to establish the fact that even postulating two different varieties of *a* still did not provide a satisfactory solution to the problem; and he postulated that in addition the language must have had a third sound, a mystery sound which was in certain respects like a vowel, but in certain respects like a consonant. Saussure could not say exactly what this mystery sound sounded like, because he thought that none of the modern European languages had a sound like it. But he claimed that it was possible to describe the mystery sound in a purely abstract way, by specifying its formal properties. These included its distinctiveness from the other vowels and consonants, its capacity to stand alone as a syllable, and its capacity to combine syllabically with vowels. This made it, in Indo-European terms, neither a consonant nor a vowel, and Saussure decided to call it a 'sonant coefficient'.

Saussure's solution, therefore, was of essentially the same order as that produced by theorists in, say, astrophysics or particle physics who may be unable to observe a body, but nevertheless predict its existence and certain of its properties by inference from the observed effects on other bodies which *can* be observed. In Saussure's case, this hypothesis turned up trumps nearly 50 years later with the decipherment of cuneiform Hittite, an Indo-European language which was found to have a phoneme with exactly the properties Saussure had specified for the mystery sound of primitive Indo-European. This was rather like having the postulated existence of a physical body confirmed by constructing more powerful telescopes or microscopes, which eventually make it visible. The point to note in the present context is Saussure's early insistence that the correct solution, however counterintuitive it might seem and however unprecedented, was to be found by treating the 'sound' as defined in relation to a system.

Wittgenstein for his part also unequivocally accepts the view that one cannot divorce verbal signs from the systems to which they belong. During the early 1930s his preferred term for the system was *calculus*. He writes:

> If you are puzzled about the nature of thought, belief, knowledge and the like, substitute for the thought the expression of the thought, etc. The difficulty which lies in this substitution, and at the same time the whole point of it, is this: the expression of belief, thought, etc. is just a sentence; — and the sentence has sense only as a member of a system of language; as one expression within a calculus. (BB:42)

Again, in the *Philosophische Grammatik* we are told: 'The meaning is the role of the word in the calculus.' (PG:63). However, he warns against construing the notion of a 'calculus' too rigidly.

> When we talk of language as a symbolism used in an exact calculus that which is in our mind can be found in the sciences and in mathematics. Our ordinary use of lan-

guage conforms to this standard of exactness only in rare cases. (BB:25)

Precisely for this reason, it seems, he abandoned the notion 'calculus' in favour of the more flexible notion 'game'. In the *Philosophische Grammatik* he uses both terms, and apparently attaches no significant difference to them:

> I can only describe language games or calculi: whether we still want to call them calculi or not doesn't much matter as long as we don't let the use of the general term divert us from examining each particular case we wish to decide. (PG:62)

Whatever we call the system, however, the essential thing is that it should *be* a system. And this means for Wittgenstein not that the signals should produce certain external effects, but that their uses should be interrelated one to another in certain characteristic ways.

> "Could a language consist simply of independent signals?" Instead of this we might ask: Are we willing to call a series of independent signs "a language"? To the question "can such a language achieve the same as one which consists of sentences, or combinations of signs?" one would have to answer: it is *experience* that will show us whether e.g. these signals have the same effect on human beings as sentences. But the effect is of no interest to us; we are looking at the phenomenon, the calculus of language. (PG:194–5)

To ask for some prior definition of systematicity here would be for Wittgenstein a futile request: for it is language which already provides the model: 'Languages *are* systems.' (PG:170). That is the point of departure, and not any purpose which having a language is deemed to serve.

> Language is not defined for us as an arrangement fulfilling a definite purpose. Rather "language" is for me a name for a collection and I understand it as including German, English, and so on, and further various systems of signs which have more or less affinity with these languages. (PG:190)

It is interesting that what Wittgenstein provides us with here corresponds more or less exactly to an informal statement of the domain which Saussure called *semiology.*

Saussure's conception of 'the system' is clearly holistic. The parts (the individual signs) cannot be divorced from the whole: for they do not exist *as signs* independently of the system. Likewise Wittgenstein emphasises that the communication systems he describes as 'language games' are to be thought of as 'complete' (BB:81, PU:2). The consequence of this is that no simple equation is possible between a sign from one system and a sign from a different system, even where the two signs happen to share the same verbal form. Thus, for example, Wittgenstein goes to some lengths to make it clear that the word *brick* in his hypothetical builder's language does not mean the same as the word *brick* in ours, *even though they are identically pronounced and even though the bricks in question are the same.* Furthermore *even though our use of the term may apparently, at least in some cases, match its use in the builder's language.*

> But don't we sometimes use the word "brick!" in just this way? Or should we say that when we use it, it is an elliptical sentence, a shorthand for "Bring me a brick"? Is it right to say that if *we* say "brick!" we *mean* "Bring me a brick"? Why should I translate the expression "brick!" into the expression "Bring me a brick"? And if they are synonymous, why shouldn't I say: If he says "brick!" he means "brick!" . . . ? Or: Why shouldn't he be able to mean just "brick!" if he is able to mean "Bring me a brick", unless you wish to assert that while he says aloud "brick!" he as a matter of fact always says in his mind, to himself, "Bring me a brick"? But what reason could we have to assert this? Suppose someone asked: If a man gives the order, "Bring me a brick", must he mean it as four words, or can't he mean it as one composite word synonymous with the one word "brick!"? (BB:78)

Wittgenstein's response to this nagging interlocutor might well have been drafted by Saussure. It runs:

> One is tempted to answer: He *means* all four words if in his language he uses that sentence in contrast with other sentences in which these words are used, such as, for instance, "Take these two bricks away". (BB:78)

But the matter is not allowed to rest there. Wittgenstein presses home the point about intrasystemic contrasts.

> But what if I asked "But how is his sentence contrasted with these others? Must he have thought them simultaneously, or shortly before or after, or is it sufficient that he should have one time learnt them, etc.?" When we have asked ourselves this question, it appears that it is irrelevant which of these alternatives is the case. And we are inclined to say that all that is really relevant is that these contrasts should exist in the system of language that he is using . . . (BB:78)

One could hardly hope for a more apposite illustration of what Saussure's followers usually took to be the central tenet of Saussurean structuralism: that contrasts within the system alone determine the values of its linguistic signs. Hence in the *Cours* it is denied, for example, that the French word *mouton* can be equated in value with the English word *sheep*, because in the former language there is no distinct word for the meat of the animal, as prepared and served for a meal. 'The difference in value between *sheep* and *mouton* hinges on the fact that in English there is also another word *mutton* for the meat, whereas *mouton* in French covers both.' (CLG:160) Similarly, the *Cours* denies that one can identify grammatical devices across different systems:

> The value of a French plural, for instance, does not match that of a Sanskrit plural, even though they often mean the same. This is because in Sanskrit, in addition to singular and plural, there is a third category of grammatical number. In Sanskrit the equivalents of expressions like *mes yeux* ('my eyes'), *mes oreilles* ('my ears'), *mes bras* ('my arms'), *mes jambes* ('my legs') would be neither in the singular nor in the plural but in the dual. It would thus be inaccurate to attribute the same value to the Sanskrit plural as to the French plural, because Sanskrit cannot use the plural in all the cases where it has to be used in French. (CLG:161)

Saussure, evidently, does not wish to claim that there is no sense in which it would be reasonable to describe uses of signs from different linguistic systems as being 'the same', as the remarks quoted above make clear. But he insists that when we do this we are adopting an 'external' point of view as our basis for comparison. If we say that there are cases where a Sanskrit plural and a French plural mean 'the same', we are looking not to their function as signs of Sanskrit and French respectively, but to something else: perhaps, for instance, to their use in translation. But translation is an activity which belongs to the domain of *parole*; and to take this as a theoretical ground for treating the French and Sanskrit plurals as having identical values would be a blatant failure to distinguish *faits de parole* from *faits de langue*. It would be to confuse system and use.

> In all these cases what we find, instead of *ideas* given in advance, are *values* emanating from a linguistic system. If we say that these values correspond to certain concepts, it must be understood that the concepts in question are purely differential. That is to say they are concepts defined not positively, in terms of their content, but negatively by contrast with other items in the same system. (CLG:162)

Where Saussure speaks of facts 'internal' to the linguistic system Wittgenstein also sometimes speaks of 'internal relations'. He maintains that *White is lighter than black* 'expresses the existence of an *internal relation*'. The picture of a black and white patch

> serves us *simultaneously* as a paradigm of what we understand by "lighter" and "darker" and as a paradigm for "white" and for "black". Now darkness 'is part of' black *inasmuch as* they are *both* represented by this patch. It is dark *by* being black. — But to put it better: it *is called* "black" and hence in our language "dark" too. That connexion, a connexion of the paradigms and the names, is set up in our language. (RFM:75–6)

For Saussure, what Wittgenstein is talking about here would be the (semantic) values of the words *black, white, dark*, etc. as established by their contrastive co-existence within the same linguistic system.

It follows for Saussure that one cannot equate signs or concepts belonging to different systems. This too finds an echo in Wittgenstein:

> We can easily imagine human beings with a 'more primitive'

logic, in which something corresponding to our negation is applied only to certain sorts of sentence; perhaps to such as do not themselves contain any negation. It would be possible to negate the proposition "He is going into the house", but a negation of the negative proposition would be meaningless, or would count only as a repetition of the negation . . .

The question whether negation had the same meaning to these people as to us would be analogous to the question whether the figure "5" meant the same to people whose numbers ended at 5 as to us. (PU:554–5)

Saussure's answer would be that "5" might have the same meaning but not the same *valeur* in the two cases. Once the 'games' perspective is adopted, it leads automatically in the direction of a Saussurean theory of values.

Is serving in badminton the same as serving in lawn tennis? Doubtless there are similarities. There must be contact between the racquet and the ball/shuttlecock, and the latter must go over the net, and so on. But there are also irreconcilable dissimilarities as regards the structure of the two games. For instance, points at badminton can be won only by the server. In Saussurean terms, the value of the service emanates from a different system in the two cases, and hence cannot be the same. Indeed, in neither case can one specify exactly what the value of the service is without explaining the whole conduct of the game in question. The *whole* conduct? Yes: because until someone is in a position to survey the whole of the game there is no assurance that all possible consequences of the service can be correctly assessed.

6

Arbitrariness

Games like chess are distinguished from many other organised human activities by combining two apparently conflicting characteristics: they are simultaneously purposeful and purposeless. That is to say, such games impose upon their players certain requirements which are compulsory but at the same time quite arbitrary. Saussure and Wittgenstein both saw this combination of features as also profoundly typical of language.

Saussure went so far as to set up 'the arbitrariness of the linguistic sign' as his 'first principle' of linguistics. In some respects this may not appear to be a very original aspect of his linguistic theorising; for few thinkers since antiquity had ever championed the Cratyline thesis that there is a 'natural correctness' in names (cf. p. 9). Although nomenclaturism had flourished in the Western tradition, it was a nomenclaturism which postulated no 'natural' connection between word and thing. Hence Saussure's 'first principle' of linguistics can easily be read as a mere confirmation of the *communis opinio* that in the debate between Cratylus and Hermogenes it was the latter whose view of language was basically right.

This interpretation of Saussurean 'arbitrariness', however, runs the risk of promoting a double conflation which seriously misrepresents the argument of the *Cours*. The conflation is on the one hand between the arbitrary and the volitional, and on the other hand between the arbitrary and the conventional. Saussure objects specifically to both assimilations. He denies that linguistic arbitrariness has anything to do with human intentions: acts of the will belong to the domain of *parole*, not to that of *langue* (CLG:30–1). He also denies that this arbitrariness is merely a matter of convention (CLG:112–13). Both these points deserve

47

careful consideration, and in Saussure's thinking they are closely connected.

(a) *Arbitrariness and volition.* For Saussure the act of speech (*parole*) is 'an individual act of the will and the intelligence' (CLG:30) in which the speaker's exercise of freedom of choice is nevertheless constrained by the possibilities available in the linguistic system (*langue*). The risk of confusion over the notion of arbitrariness arises here because, for example, saying 'The dog bit the postman' rather than 'The postman was bitten by the dog' might be described as an 'arbitrary' decision *made by the speaker.* The use of the term 'arbitrary' in this kind of case brings to the fore the notion of a more or less random choice, implying that, in relation to what the speaker wanted to say, it would have made no (great) difference which of the two sentences was uttered. For Saussure, however, the speaker's decision is volitional, not arbitrary. What is arbitrary is the relationship *between the two sentences*: more exactly, for Saussure that relationship will fall into the category of the 'relatively arbitrary' (see p. 53). This arbitrary relationship emanates from the linguistic system, and is not in any way determined or affected by the choices made by speakers, either individually or collectively. Saussure insists that the signs of *la langue* are not under the control of the linguistic community, even though they are maintained or not maintained in existence by nothing else but the volitional activity of *parole*; and this strikes him as one of the most paradoxical aspects of language.

> The signal, in relation to the idea it represents, may seem to be freely chosen. However, from the point of view of the linguistic community, the signal is imposed rather than freely chosen. Speakers are not consulted about its choice. Once the language has selected a signal, it cannot be freely replaced by any other. There appears to be something rather contradictory about this. It is a kind of linguistic Hobson's choice. What can be chosen is already determined in advance. No individual is able, even if he wished, to modify in any way a choice already established in the language. Nor can the linguistic community exercise its authority to change even a single word. The community, as much as the individual, is bound to its language. (CLG:104)

(b) *Arbitrariness and conventionality.* Although the use of the term is perhaps not entirely consistent throughout the *Cours*, it is evident that Saussure is reluctant to concede that the institution of *la langue* is merely or entirely conventional. This is because for Saussure the notion of convention, unless further qualified, generally implies a practice which people are free to adopt, adapt, flout, or change by mutual agreement; furthermore, a practice in which there is an element of the rational and the non-arbitrary. Conventions can be decided on in order to suit the interests of the parties concerned: but this is never, for Saussure, characteristic of the establishment of a linguistic sign. And although it is perfectly possible to set up whole communication systems by convention, this is not in fact the case with *la langue*.

Languages as we find them operating in human society are not in any sense the products of human decisions to establish them in the form in which we find them. In order to characterise languages correctly, says Saussure, we need to take into account simultaneously three factors belonging to quite different orders of consideration. First, as regards the individual, a language is 'the whole set of linguistic habits which enable the speaker to understand and to make himself understood' (CLG:112). But this cannot stand as an adequate definition since it fails to relate the language to social reality. For 'in order to have a language, there must be a *community of speakers*' (CLG:112). This is the second factor to be recognised. But incorporating the social factor still leaves an important gap in the account, for the following reason.

> Since the linguistic sign is arbitrary, a language as so far defined would appear to be an adaptable system, which can be organised in any way one likes, and is based solely upon a principle of rationality. Its social nature, as such, is not incompatible with this view. Social psychology, doubtless, must operate on more than a purely logical basis: account must be taken of everything which might affect the operation of reason in practical relations between one individual and another. But that is not the objection to regarding a language as a mere convention, which can be modified to suit the interests of those involved. There is something else. We must consider what is brought about by the passage of time, as well as what is brought about by the forces of social integration. Without taking into account the contribution of time, our grasp of linguistic reality remains incomplete. (CLG:112–13)

49

In other words, we cannot hope to explain why the *faits de langue* in any given case are as they are merely by appeal to their 'conventional' nature. That would be to confuse, for example, (i) accounting for why *Good morning* is used as a greeting, with (ii) accounting for why the words for 'good' and 'morning' are respectively *good* and *morning*. For the latter there can be no satisfactory explanation which does not appeal to historical considerations. Or else we simply have to say that there is no explanation. Whereas given the words *good* and *morning*, it does not take much ingenuity to construct a more or less plausible social rationale for the convention of greeting people by saying 'Good morning'. The convention would not, in Saussurean terms, be arbitrary: unlike the words which the convention makes use of. Conventionality, on this view, relates to society's communicational use of the materials supplied by *la langue*, while arbitrariness concerns the internal relations of *la langue*. Or, perhaps more exactly, conventionality is a question of the freedom of choice available to the linguistic community, whereas arbitrariness is a question of the freedom of choice available to the language.

* * *

Before pursuing Saussure's line of thought further, a preliminary comparison with Wittgenstein is in order. Wittgenstein is often described as a 'conventionalist', although it is misleading to use that label to assimilate his position to the 'conventionalism' of the Vienna Circle (Baker and Hacker 1985:338–47). In any case, the debate over Wittgenstein's 'conventionalism' has more to do with his philosophy of logic and mathematics than with his view of how ordinary language works. Wittgenstein holds that all languages are founded on convention (*Übereinkunft*), including, as he revealingly remarks, the 'language' of our sense impressions (PU:355). Here, if anywhere, one might expect that even a Hermogenes would concede a 'natural' link between sign and meaning. For Wittgenstein, however, the reason why we take our sense impressions to give us reliable information (e.g. that it is raining) is that experience has taught us to rely on certain connections between sense impressions and conditions in the external world. Although the connections may be natural, our interpretation of them as reliable indices is 'conventional'. If this is a correct construal of Wittgenstein's remark concerning the 'language' of sense-impressions, then a language like English can be seen as a man-made second-order extension of the 'natural conventions' on which all living creatures rely.

Wittgenstein would doubtless have agreed with everything Saussure says concerning the individual's powerlessness to alter *faits de langue* (linguistic conventions) by an act of will. This, precisely, is the point of the challenge in PU:510 to '*say* "It's cold here" and *mean* "It's warm here" '. Any attempt to meet this challenge will be self-defeating in the sense that it will consist in the mental gymnastics of uttering certain words while trying to 'think' or internally activate a meaning associated with certain other words. This merely strains the muscles of the imagination and thereby drives painfully home the lesson that no individual, by a mere effort of volition, can do anything about the meaning of *It's cold here.*

But could not Wittgenstein's challenge be met without risk of mental strain as follows? The sceptic says, 'When I next utter the words "It's cold here" they are to be taken as meaning "It's warm here." Now listen carefully. "It's cold here." ' This stipulation does not appear to violate any 'rules of English'. It is comprehensible. (And if the hearer complains that the utterance 'It's cold here' still sounded as if it meant 'It's cold here', and not as if it meant 'It's warm here', the sceptic is entitled to complain that the explicit instructions accompanying the experiment have been disregarded.) Wittgenstein at one point seems to invite the above manoeuvre: 'I say the sentence: "The weather is fine"; but the words are after all arbitrary signs — so let's put "a b c d" in their place.' (PU:508) However, one may well ask what Wittgenstein means here by 'arbitrary'.

Wittgenstein would no more wish to deny than Saussure the general possibility of stipulating a meaning for a sign. ('Let *x* be 22 and *y* be 11.' 'When I wave my handkerchief, that means "Ignite the fuse." ') So is the objection to 'It's cold here' meaning 'It's warm here' that one cannot stipulate a new meaning for a sign that already has one? Presumably not. What exactly, then, is the objection?

First, stipulating a new meaning should not be confused with altering the old meaning. Indeed, in order to make sense of the stipulation itself it has to be supposed that, notwithstanding the proposed innovation, the old meaning is somehow still in place. In Saussurean terms, the old meaning of *It's warm here* is defined by its opposition within the system to, *inter alia*, the meaning of

It's cold here. So the stipulation, as an act of *parole*, risks self-stultification if it is interpreted as *eo ipso* altering the system.

Second, an alteration of the system would in any case involve much more than a new meaning for one sentence. 'Can I say "bububu" and mean "If it doesn't rain I shall go for a walk"? — It is only in a language that I can mean something by something.' (PU:p.18) In order to say *bububu* and mean 'If it doesn't rain I shall go for a walk', then, I must first find a language in which *bububu* means just that. But, as far as we know, there is no such language; any more than there is a language in which *It's cold here* means 'It's warm here'. Wait a minute. Haven't we now come round again to denying the very possibility of establishing a new sign by stipulation?

Wittgenstein admits that when we first substitute one set of arbitrary signs for another set (*a, b, c, d* for *The weather is fine*) we may at first have some difficulty in connecting the new set with the meanings of the old set.

> I am not used, I might say, to saying "a" instead of "the", "b" instead of "weather", etc. But I don't mean by that that I am not used to making an immediate association between the word "the" and "a", but that I am not used to using "a" *in the place* of "the" — and therefore in the sense of "the". (I have not mastered this language.) (PU:508)

But the obvious riposte here to 'I have not mastered this language' is: 'What language?' As in the case of *bububu*, where is the language in which *a* means 'the', *b* means 'weather', and so on? If there is no such language, then we must have been deceiving ourselves when we thought we could just substitute one set of arbitrary signs for another.

Here one glimpses the iceberg tip of submerged problems about linguistic innovation which, arguably, are never satisfactorily dealt with either in the *Cours* or in the *Philosophische Untersuchungen* (cf. Chapter 8). All that need be pointed out for the moment is the connection between arbitrariness and linguistic change, which Saussure sees but Wittgenstein ignores. This connection is quite crucial to Saussure's account of the intermeshing between synchronic and diachronic linguistics. For

> to say that a language is the product of social forces does not automatically explain why it comes to be constrained

in the way it is. Bearing in mind that a language is always an inheritance from the past, one must add that the social forces in question act over a period of time. If stability is a characteristic of languages, it is not only because languages are anchored in the community. They are also anchored in time. The two factors are inseparable. Continuity with the past constantly restricts freedom of choice. If the Frenchman of today uses words like *homme* ('man') and *chien* ('dog'), it is because these words were used by his forefathers. Ultimately there is a connexion between these two opposing factors: the arbitrary convention which allows free choice, and the passage of time, which fixes that choice. It is because the linguistic sign is arbitrary that it knows no other law than that of tradition, and because it is founded upon tradition that it can be arbitrary. (CLG:108)

* * *

Saussure distinguishes two kinds of arbitrariness, which he terms 'absolute' and 'relative'. Signs which belong to the former class are 'unmotivated', and to the latter class 'motivated'. He maintains that: 'There exists no language in which nothing at all is motivated. Even to conceive of such a language is an impossibility by definition.' (CLG:183) Clearly Saussure is not thinking here of 'languages' like the one used by Wittgenstein's builder and his assistant. This, it might be argued, contains no motivated feature of any kind, and precisely for that reason Saussure would presumably have refused to count it as a language. A related point is sometimes made by critics who feel that a major lacuna in the later Wittgenstein's discussions of language is that the concentration on 'primitive', over-simple language games creates a blind spot where syntax is concerned. Of the builder's language, Kenny writes:

One might, however, be inclined to object that unless a language-game is at least complicated enough to allow a distinction between words and sentences to be drawn, then it does not really deserve to be called a *language*-game at all. Wittgenstein was surely right in thinking when he wrote the *Tractatus* that the articulation of propositions, and the possibility of expressing a new sense with old words, is something crucial for the understanding of language. It is not at all clear that the language-game in which the builders call out 'block', 'pillar' and 'stone' to each other could be, as Wittgenstein says it could, 'a complete primitive language'. (Kenny 1973:168–9)

To conclude that here we see an important gap opening up between Saussure's view of language and Wittgenstein's would, however, be too hasty. For Saussure does not insist that in a language at least some of the vocabulary must be motivated: what he says is impossible is a language in which 'nothing at all is motivated'. He illustrates the difference between motivation and its absence by reference to the French numeral system.

The French word *vingt* ('twenty') is unmotivated, whereas *dix-neuf* ('nineteen') is not unmotivated to the same extent. For *dix-neuf* evokes the words of which it is composed, *dix* ('ten') and *neuf* ('nine'), and those of the same numerical series: *dix* ('ten'), *neuf* ('nine'), *vingt-neuf* ('twenty-nine'), *dix-huit* ('eighteen'), *soixante-dix* ('seventy'), etc. Taken individually, *dix* and *neuf* are on the same footing as *vingt*, but *dix-neuf* is an example of relative motivation. (CLG:181)

From this it is clear that Saussure would only regard as totally unmotivated a set of number-words in which the designations were as formally unrelated as *dix* is to *neuf* or *vingt* to *dix*. But such a set would not constitute a numeral *system*, in the sense that the term for each cardinal number from 'one' to infinity would have to be separately learnt. Saussure's general point is that no set of signs constituting a language is structured like that. The characteristic feature of *linguistic* structure is combinatorial systematicity of some kind. But it is worth noting that this does not follow automatically from Saussure's twin principles of linguistics (the 'principle of arbitrariness' and the 'principle of linearity'). There is for him no contradiction in the notion of a semiological system in which the signs are both linear and 'absolutely' arbitrary. His point is that we cannot seriously entertain the notion that such a system (or even a combination of such systems) could function adequately as a language in the sense in which French and English are languages; that is, as all-purpose communication systems for the multifarious needs of any community of living beings like ourselves.

In Saussurean terms, the individual words of the language

described in PU:2 are all unmotivated, being syntagmatically unanalysable. We should note, however, that Wittgenstein specifically makes the point that the builder's assistant has to bring the stones in the order in which the builder requires them. So, arguably, the system does have a syntagmatic dimension after all, which Wittgenstein simply takes for granted. In other words, the order in which the builder utters the words corresponds to the order in which he needs the stones. Sequence is not, therefore, without significance.

But is this, it may be asked, syntax? The question is more complex than at first sight appears (which supports Wittgenstein's claim that consideration of very primitive language games may enlighten us in unsuspected ways). Wittgenstein elsewhere cites ironically the story of the French politician who claimed that in French sentences the words occur in the sequence in which the ideas occur to the speaker (PG:107). Would it be something like the obverse of this mistake to treat the builder's word-sequences as sentences?

To focus clearly upon the relevant theoretical issue here, it may be helpful to disengage it from a tangle of adjacent irrelevancies. First, the question has nothing to do with the mechanics or the psychology of speech production. Perhaps Wittgenstein's builder works at a rather leisurely pace and utters no more than one word every five minutes or so. Perhaps his method of working allows him great flexibility in the order of operations, with the result that when he utters one word he may not know what the next word will be. In everyday speech, our sentences do not have five-minute gaps between each word, even though we may sometimes begin a sentence without knowing how it is going to end. Syntagmatics, nevertheless, does not depend on speed of utterance, discourse planning strategies, or factors of that order. Syntagmatic structure is no more time-bound than the structure of a painting or drawing. I can continue today the sentence I began to write six months ago, just as I can complete next week the sketch begun on holiday last summer. How do I know it is the same sentence? As reliably or unreliably as I know it is the same sketch.

Second, the issue cannot be resolved by simple comparison between the builder's utterances and corresponding utterances in German or English. Wittgenstein himself makes this point (PU:19, 20). To argue that 'Block!' is equivalent to 'Bring me a block!', and therefore counts as a complete sentence is simply to foist the familiar structure of English upon a communication system which manifestly has no such structure. In any case, nothing obliges us to accept a one-to-one correlation between commands and sentences. (No grammarian argues that 'Stand up, speak up and shut up' must be three sentences because it expresses three commands.)

Third, it might perhaps be urged that no language can have syntagmatic structure which has only one part of speech. But this seems to be a disguised version of the objection which counts each command as a separate sentence. Suppose Wittgenstein had enriched the builder's vocabulary with the addition of the word *and*, specifying that this word is used occasionally (and optionally) in between any two consecutive utterances of the other four words. The assistant proceeds in the same way, regardless of whether *and* is used or not. The objection against systems with only one part of speech is now met; for this enriched system has a 'conjunction'. But would this communicationally pointless embellishment at one stroke transform a four-word non-language into a five-word language, equipped with 'genuine' sentence-structure? Would there now be a syntactic basis for distinguishing and classifying 'constructions'?

No objection based on considerations of the kind so far examined will carry much weight against the positive case which can be constructed along strictly Saussurean lines. It will run as follows. If the builder's language described by Wittgenstein is construed as a sign system governed by Saussure's principle of linearity, as it seems to be, then the crucial question is whether relations of linearity within the system are communicationally relevant. Do changes of order 'change the message'? The answer to this is unequivocally 'Yes'. Furthermore, that the relevant features of linearity are indeed part of the system, and not externally imposed, can be demonstrated by contrasting the system as described in PU:2 with other possible systems using the same verbal units. For example, the arrangement might have been that when the builder uttered the word 'Block!' followed by the word 'Slab!' his assistant was to bring the block and the slab in reverse order. Clearly, the difference between this system and the one described by Wittgenstein is a difference of syntagmatics: for nothing has changed in the correlation of the words *block* with blocks, *slab* with slabs, etc. It follows from this that both systems have a syntagmatic dimension, and furthermore a syntagmatics in which sequential ordering of words is motivated. (It is still arbitrary, however, in that these are merely two out of indefinitely many possibilities for using contrasts of linearity within the system in order to ensure that the assistant brings the items to the builder in the desired order.)

It should be stressed that this does not involve equating motivation with significance, any more than in Saussure's account of *dix-neuf*. The individual signs in the syntagma are unmotivated; but the syntagma itself is not. However, Saussure does not say that the *entire* syntagma is motivated: it would still be motivated if the French for 'nineteen' were *neuf-dix*. So the order of elements, as well as the individual signs in this composite whole, remain 'absolutely' arbitrary. Nineteen is not 'ten plus nine' rather than 'nine plus ten'. Motivation, in other words, is not to be confused with regularity of patterning. Throughout the compound French numerals from 1 to 100, the rule is that 'tens precede units': the pattern is always of the type *dix-neuf*, never of the type *neuf-dix*. In that sense, the order of elements is not random, but it is unmotivated all the same.

The essential point about Saussurean 'motivation' is that the question does not arise except at the syntagmatic level. Individual signs are never motivated. One cannot cite even a hypothetical example of what such a sign would be like. How, for instance, could one alter the French numeral *neuf* so that it should still mean 'nine' and yet (i) acquire motivation, and (ii) remain a single sign? To see that this is an impossibility is to grasp something fundamental to Saussure's concept of arbitrariness. It is, at the same time, to grasp why one cannot deny *a priori* to Wittgenstein's builder's language a syntagmatic dimension. To be sure, the system presented in PU:2 is underdescribed. For a complete analysis one would need to know much more about the constructional enterprise. Is the assistant strong enough to carry more than one item at a time? Is the builder sufficiently far-sighted to predict how many items he will need in the next three hours? More questions would need to be asked and answered (at least if the present construal of Wittgenstein's thinking is correct). For what is at issue affects both (i) what is determined by 'grammar' (see Chapter 7), and (ii) what is meant by 'communication' (see Chapter 9). But to deny Wittgenstein's builder a syntagmatics of discourse is, implicitly, to accuse Wittgenstein of drawing an arbitrary line between what is 'in' a language and what lies 'outside'. And this is the very last accusation which can plausibly be levelled at someone who is ready to welcome such a catholic use of the term *language* as Wittgenstein.

For Saussure there is an intimate link between arbitrariness and linguistic structure. It would be no exaggeration, indeed, to say that for Saussure linguistic structure is *constituted by* limitations on arbitrariness, both in syntagmatic and in associative relations.

> Everything having to do with languages as systems needs to be approached, we are convinced, with a view to examining the limitations of arbitrariness. It is an approach which linguists have neglected. But it offers the best possible basis for linguistic studies. For the entire linguistic system is founded upon the irrational principle that the sign is arbitrary. Applied without restriction, the principle would lead to utter chaos. But the mind succeeds in introducing a principle of order and regularity into certain areas of the mass of signs. This is the role of relative motivation. If languages had a mechanism which were entirely rational, that mechanism could be studied in its own right. But it provides only a partial correction to a system which is chaotic by nature. Hence we must adopt the point of view demanded by the nature of linguistic structure itself, and study this mechanism as a way of imposing a limitation upon what is arbitrary. (CLG:182–3)

Wittgenstein does not express himself in similar terms; but his position is nevertheless very close to Saussure's here. Just how close can again be illustrated by reference to the builder's language of PU:2. Why, we may ask, does Wittgenstein stipulate that the building materials are to be brought in the order in which the builder needs them? To answer that question, let us suppose that the builder's assistant falls ill and is replaced by a foreign immigrant worker. The builder assumes that his new assistant understands the language. In fact he does not, but hopes to be able to bluff his way through. What will happen in this situation?

Let us further suppose, in order to clarify the example, that builder and assistant are not in visual contact. So there is no way the builder can indicate what he needs by pointing at the object. Imagine that the builder calls down a lift shaft, and the assistant has to send up what is called for. We may grant that the new assistant has at least grasped that his job is to send up the items the builder needs; but he simply does not know which word corresponds to which of the four types of building material available in the store. So he reasons that sooner or later the builder will need all four, and therefore it does not matter which order they arrive in, provided he keeps the builder supplied with a reasonable selection. Therefore, when the builder calls, the assistant simply fetches an item from one of the four piles at random. (Perhaps he has other tasks to occupy him at the bottom of the lift shaft while awaiting the builder's instructions.)

What will the builder's strategy be in this situation? He will soon discover that when he shouts 'Block!' down the lift shaft he has only a one-in-four chance of getting one. So if a slab arrives when he calls 'Block!' he simply puts it on one side and calls 'Block!' again, until eventually a block arrives. The next time he needs a slab he does not need to call 'Slab!' because he already has to hand the slab he obtained by calling 'Block!'. And so on. Having adjusted to this new situation, the builder finds that he can carry on much as usual.

In this new situation, communication of sorts is still taking place; but it is no longer the system the builder used with his previous assistant. In effect, all that has been abandoned is the requirement that the materials are fetched in the order in which the builder needs them. But the result of abandoning this requirement is that in practice there is no longer any communicational correspondence between *block* and blocks, *slab* and slabs, etc. There may still be a correspondence in the builder's mind: but, as Wittgenstein would be the first to point out, that is a very different matter. In the communication system itself those correlations have broken down.

What does it mean to say that the correlations have broken down? It means that the domain of the arbitrary has been drastically increased. Whereas formerly it made an important difference whether the builder called 'Block!' or 'Slab!' or 'Pillar!' or 'Beam!', now it makes no difference at all. It is, in fact, completely arbitrary. If the builder continues to shout 'Block!' when he needs a block, that will simply be by force of habit. He will stand just as much chance of getting a block if he shouts 'Beam!'.

The contrast between the old situation and the new one brings out an important point. Wittgenstein's stipulation about the order of items to be fetched is not superfluous: it holds the key to what Saussure would call the 'limitation of the arbitrary' in the builder's language. For without it the structure of the entire communication system collapses. In other words, syntagmatics and sign-class are mutually dependent. Unlimited arbitrariness equals linguistic chaos: and this must inevitably be so if languages, like games, have nothing in the world 'outside' to secure and shore up their internal organisation.

Again, this conclusion follows inevitably once language is viewed from a 'games' perspective. The rules governing the moves of the pieces in chess are restrictions on the arbitrariness of allowing them to move in whatever fashion the players choose. But now consider the following proposal for increasing the arbitrariness of chess: let all the pieces move as in the standard game except the knight, which shall be allowed to move without any restrictions at all. Any campaign for the reform of chess which advocated this proposal would in effect be advocating the abolition of chess. *Not* because the result would be a different game; but because it would be no game at all. To allow the knight unlimited freedom of manoeuvre while insisting that the other pieces keep their traditional moves takes us from the realm of the playable into the realm of the unplayable. In that sense too signs and syntagmatics are systematically interlocked.

7

Grammar

Both Saussure and Wittgenstein came to use the traditional term *grammar* in an apparently very untraditional manner. It might be said of both that they were responsible for reorienting its use in ways which left a lasting mark upon the twentieth century's view of language. In both cases the notion of 'grammar' which appears in their work is closely related to that of 'arbitrariness' and to the idea that languages are in many respects like games played according to rules. Saussure was very much aware of the clash between his notion of grammar and the more usual current notion; Wittgenstein apparently was not, even though it was pointed out to him.

* * *

Grammar in the Western tradition was originally connected with the introduction of writing.

> That the development and use of writing was the first piece of linguistic scholarship in Greece is attested by the history of the word *grammatikos*; up to and including the time of Plato and Aristotle the word meant simply one who understood the use of letters, *grammata*, and could read and write, and *technē grammatikē* was the skill of reading and writing. (Robins 1979:13)

Grammar later developed as a central component of the Graeco-Roman educational curriculum and covered a much broader range of topics than in modern times. The grammarian of Quintilian's day was a specialist teacher, whose brief was to make his pupils

61

fully literate, in particular by introducing them to the study of great literary works. The early grammatical treatise attributed to Dionysius Thrax mentions six divisions of grammar, of which the most important is said to be 'the appreciation of literary compositions' (Robins 1979:31).

By the middle ages, however, the province of grammar had been drastically reduced. It had been promoted in importance to the status of a university subject, being one of the branches of the trivium, ranked alongside logic and rhetoric; but its content had shrunk. Grammar was to all intents and purposes what was set out in the two most famous grammar books of antiquity; the Latin grammars of Priscian and Donatus. The notion of the 'grammar' of any non-Classical language was simply not entertained, and since Priscian and Donatus were neither phoneticians nor lexicographers, medieval grammar was in effect simply Latin morphology and syntax.

Over the following centuries, as the countries of Europe gradually acquired bodies of vernacular literature of their own, and Latin began to lose ground as the international language of learning, politics and religion, the idea took hold that grammarians ought to perform for the vernacular languages the service which Priscian and Donatus were taken to have performed for Latin: namely, to 'fix the rules' once and for all. This need was particularly felt at a time when linguistic uniformity was conspicuous by its absence, and conflicting idioms and dialect forms vied with one another. From the Renaissance onwards, to have an authoritatively 'regulated' language came increasingly to be a desideratum for any country which aspired to full 'national' status in the affairs of Europe. In this climate of opinion, the most important role of the grammarian came to be seen as that of linguistic legislator, and grammar to be viewed as the product of his legislation.

A distinction which acquires particular importance in this 'legislative' context is that between grammar and 'usage'. Usage is not automatically 'grammatical', even though it may be current and well established. On the contrary, if established usage were always correct, then the grammarian would be out of business. It is usage which has to conform to grammar in order to be correct; and not grammar which has to conform to usage in order to be correct. The purpose of grammatical instruction is, precisely, to teach people which of the usages they may be familiar with are correct and which are not. Grammar pursued on the basis and in the spirit of these assumptions came later to be called 'normative grammar' or 'prescriptive grammar' (to distinguish it from a quite different conceptualisation of the subject). It is also what is sometimes taken to be implied, although misleadingly so, by the term 'traditional grammar'. (For not all traditional grammar was normative, nor was all normative grammar traditional.)

Normative grammarians at various times sought to justify their prescriptive pronouncements concerning correct usage by reference to logical distinctions, in turn treated as explicable by reference to universal operations of the human mind. This form of justification goes back to the medieval *modistae*, who sought to 'explain' language philosophically as a rational system of expression, and ultimately has Aristotelian roots; but it became especially common in the sixteenth and seventeenth centuries. A frequent assumption made by grammarians of the period is that underneath the particular grammar of any individual language there lies a 'general grammar' or 'universal grammar' common to the whole of mankind. Within this rationalist perspective, the 'best' language tends to be seen as one in which usage most conspicuously reflects the principles of general grammar. This in turn leads to the idea that it should be possible to construct an ideal language, based on universal grammar. Attempts to devise such systems (variously referred to as 'universal languages', 'philosophical languages' or 'real characters') feature prominently in the intellectual activity associated with the birth and advancement of the natural sciences in their modern academic form.

A reaction against the normative and rationalistic preoccupations of the preceding period gathered momentum during the course of the nineteenth century. It was ushered in by the study of the 'comparative grammar' of the Indo-European languages. For the comparativists grammar was essentially a complex of phonological, morphological and syntactic patterns which could be inferred from the evidence of attested usage, whether of living languages or of those no longer spoken. The grammar of any language, on this view, could be discovered or reconstructed without access to the pronouncements of its grammarians (if any) and without reliance on any assumed principles of general grammar, provided the scholar had available a sufficient body of evidence in the form of written texts or transcriptions, preferably covering a group of genealogically related languages or chronologically successive varieties of the same language. This approach to grammar, widely regarded as the only 'scientific' basis for grammatical studies, came to be designated 'descriptive' (a term generally interpreted as implying both a rejection of normative viewpoints and a deliberate agnosticism concerning the possibility of rationalistic elucidations of linguistic structure). Grammar is thus seen as merely part of a continuously evolving matrix of communicational behaviour, shaped by factors which largely elude the subjective grasp of members of the linguistic community and become apparent only to the objective eye of the historian. Accordingly, the only 'scientific' explanation of a grammatical fact is a historical explanation.

* * *

The historical background sketched above is the minimum required to understand what lies behind the various remarks about grammar and grammarians scattered throughout the *Cours*. When Saussure describes the sole aim of grammar as 'providing rules which distinguish between correct and incorrect forms' and castigates the grammarian's approach as unscientific (CLG:13) his target is normative grammar. When he denies the reality of 'historical grammar' (CLG:185) his target is the concept of grammar espoused by the comparativists and their successors. When he complains that linguistics 'is always working with concepts originally introduced by the grammarians' (CLG:153) he has in mind the traditional parts-of-speech system and the associated terminology which goes back to Dionysius Thrax. His generalisations about the history of grammar are sweeping and his assimilation of 'traditional grammar' to normative grammar (CLG:118) is crude. But it would be folly to put these shortcomings down to Saussure's ignorance, as has sometimes been suggested: a scholar who had spent his entire career in the field of Indo-European studies, and was equally at home with the Sanskrit grammarians as with those of Greece and Rome, is unlikely to have known no better. Saussure's dismissive observations about grammar have to be construed as part of a polemic which draws its rationale from Saussure's own 'Copernican' revolution in linguistics, and must be set against what Saussure proposes as the right way to view grammar.

The normative grammarian, the universal grammarian and the comparativist have all, in Saussure's estimation, made one error in common. They have mistaken for grammar something which is not grammar, but which is derived from grammar. They have confused grammar with its by-products. This confusion takes a different form in the three separate cases. The normative grammarian confuses grammatical facts with value judgements based upon those facts, a confusion arising in part from setting one usage against another in competition for social superiority. The universal grammarian confuses grammatical facts with logical or psychological operations which make use of those facts, thus attempting misguidedly to reduce the irreducible differences between one language and another. The comparative grammarian confuses grammatical facts with the historical regularities which emerge over time as a result of grammar. All three, in short, fail to distinguish *langue* from *parole*, albeit in different ways and with different consequences. These consequences have no common result, other than being inimical to, and indeed quite disastrous for, the establishment of a true science of language.

Saussure's concept of grammar is the keystone of linguistic structuralism. Grammar is essentially synchronic. For any given language, at any given stage in its history, the totality of structural synchronic facts constitutes its grammar. That is why for Saussure grammatical facts embrace a far wider range than was traditionally subsumed under the term *grammar*: in particular, grammatical facts are not merely those of morphology and syntax (a distinction which in any case Saussure rejects). It is also why Saussure will have no talk of 'historical grammar': for grammar, being synchronic in nature, cannot embrace relations obtaining across historically separate systems. One grammar does not over time 'change into' another grammar: nor do two chronologically successive grammars somehow comprise historical variants of one and the same grammar.

Grammar has a status analogous to the constitution of a game. If the components and the rules are different, we are playing a different game, even though both may go under the same name. Although it may be possible to trace historical connections between different games, all called 'chess', there is no historical amalgam of these which is itself 'the' game in question. On the contrary, such an amalgam is not a game at all: it cannot be played because it comprises a hotchpotch of conflicting rules. Similarly, no one can speak Latin and French simultaneously:

nor is there any language of which Latin grammar and French grammar are simply alternative versions.

* * *

Wittgenstein, like Saussure, refused to limit the term *grammar* to its run-of-the-mill applications. 'Unusual and idiosyncratic' (Baker and Hacker 1980:xix) is a phlegmatic description of the way he employs it in his arguments about language. Other philosophers (Moore, Waismann) found this disconcerting and said so. A less charitable verdict might be that Wittgenstein distorts what is ordinarily understood by *grammar* out of all recognition. While some of his appeals to grammar (for instance, his talk of the 'grammar' of a concept) can readily be understood as straightforwardly metaphorical (a projection from the grammar of a corresponding word or words), other pronouncements can hardly fail to bring his reader up short, and were presumably intended to do so. One does not at first sight know what to make of a generalisation such as

> *Essence* is expressed by grammar. (PU:371)

or

> Grammar tells us what kind of object anything is. (PU:373)

or

> Whether a proposition entails another proposition must be clear from the grammar of the proposition and from that alone. (PG:256)

In such cases, as with Saussure, it appears that we are parting company with what we may have thought the word *grammar* meant, and are forced to acknowledge that the word has been boldly appropriated for polemic purposes by a theorist who is concerned to jolt us out of the rut of linguistic *idées reçues*.

Wittgenstein also made use of grammatical terminology in novel ways. For example, the expression *parts of speech*: 'in ordinary grammar one might as well distinguish "shape words", "colour words", "sound words", "substance words" and so on as different parts of speech.' (PG:61) Thus *ellipse, circle, square,* etc. would belong to a different part of speech from *red, yellow, green,* etc. Correspondingly, '*Ellipse' is a shape word* would be like '*Ellipse' is a noun*. Wittgenstein writes as if this failure to subclassify parts of speech further were simply the result of oversight — or oversimplification — on the part of grammarians.

Did Wittgenstein, like Saussure, use the term *grammar* in a deliberately iconoclastic manner? Some commentators doubt it.

> Was Wittgenstein stretching the concept of grammar, or even introducing a different concept of grammar? He firmly denied this . . . Was Wittgenstein stretching the concept of a rule or rules of grammar? Again, there is no evidence to suggest that he thought so. (Hacker 1986:182)

Against this, however, has to be set the fact that Wittgenstein himself occasionally speaks of 'ordinary grammar' (as in PG:61, quoted above). One might ask why a writer feels the need to use an expression such as *ordinary grammar* at all unless he realises that much of the time he is speaking of not-so-ordinary grammar. Or why he needs to distinguish (in advance of any generative grammarian) between 'deep' and 'surface' grammar (*Tiefengrammatik* versus *Oberflächengrammatik*)?

> In the use of words one might distinguish 'surface grammar' from 'depth grammar'. What immediately impresses itself upon us about the use of a word is the way it is used in the construction of the sentence, the part of its use — one might say — that can be taken in by the ear. — And now compare the depth grammar, say of the word "to mean", with what its surface grammar would lead us to suspect. No wonder we find it difficult to know our way about. (PU:664)

From this it seems clear that most of Wittgenstein's remarks about grammar concern 'depth grammar': and whatever 'depth grammar' may be, it is certainly not the 'ordinary grammar' of the grammar books.

Finally, when a philosopher writes, 'Since time and the truth-functions taste so different, and since they manifest their nature only and wholly in grammar, it is grammar that must explain the different taste' (PG:216), it is difficult to believe that he is not consciously playing ducks and drakes with our everyday notions of what grammar is.

Be that as it may, and whatever doubts one may have about how 'depth grammar' relates to ordinary grammar, no doubt need be entertained concerning Wittgenstein's readiness to see the rules of a game as having a 'grammatical' character.

> Grammar describes the use of words in the language.
> So it has somewhat the same relation to the language as the description of a game, the rules of a game, have to the game. (PG:60)

('Grammar', we may note, and 'rules' are here envisaged as descriptions.) Similarly, when he says, ' "I can use the word 'yellow' " is like "I know how to move the king in chess" ' (PG:49), there is no doubt that, in so far as knowing how to move the king is knowing how to move it in accordance with the rules, we are being invited to see the use of the word *yellow* as being determined by the rules (i.e. the grammar) of the language.

Therefore for Wittgenstein, as for Saussure, it makes no sense to exclude vocabulary and semantics from the domain of grammar. Nor do morphological and syntactic phenomena occupy any privileged position within that domain. Once we see that the combinatorial possibilities characteristic of the deployment of a word are not independent of what the word means, any distinction between two separate sets of rules governing its use becomes at best an expository convenience and at worst a misleading dichotomy. Wittgenstein argues:

> One is inclined to make a distinction between rules of grammar that set up "a connection between language and reality" and those that do not. A rule of the first kind is "this colour is called 'red' ", — a rule of the second kind is "$\sim\sim p = p$". With regard to this distinction there is a common error; language is not something that is first given a structure and then fitted on to reality. (PG:89)

Saussure might have made the corresponding point in his own terms by saying: 'Languages are not first equipped with a syntagmatics and only then provided with signs.' (A version of the same mistake was later made by those generative grammarians who insisted that in English, French, Latin, etc., syntax can be treated as 'autonomous'.) As Wittgenstein remarks: 'the sign does its job only in a grammatical system'. (PG:87) But this is not to be construed as implying that signs and grammar are two separate components, the latter providing the empty slots into which the former fit. On the contrary, a sign is itself part of the grammar of a language.

* * *

In both Wittgenstein and Saussure discussion of grammar is bound up in various ways with discussion of rules; although more inextricably in Wittgenstein's case than in Saussure's. The concept 'rule' is one of the main links in the analogy between languages and games. Without it the analogy would limp badly, or break down altogether. At the same time, it is a vulnerable link, and one which gives rise to problems for both thinkers.

The expressions *grammar, game, rule, rule of grammar* and *rule of the game* have their counterparts in all major European languages, and this is part of the general cultural inheritance which both Saussure and Wittgenstein simply take for granted. To translate either the *Cours* or the *Philosophische Untersuchungen* into a language which lacked anything corresponding to that particular nexus of words would pose severe problems: far more severe than the translation problems occasioned by the fact that not all European languages have obvious lexical twins matching the French pair *langage* and *langue*, or the fact that not all European languages have a single word as implacably monolithic as the German *Satz*. These latter problems are bad enough. But the conundrum involving the *rule-grammar-game* complex would be infinitely worse. To point to that conundrum would be a sufficient answer if one were challenged to give an example of the respects in which Saussure and Wittgenstein are both (to use Whorfian terminology) 'Standard Average European' thinkers.

Various features of the ways in which both Saussure and Wittgenstein use terms like *grammar* and *rule* come from this common background. Neither, for example, draws a clear and consistent terminological distinction between (i) the sense in which grammars and rules are what may be produced in response to questions about how to play games or use words, and (ii) the sense in which grammars and rules are not those answers as such but whatever it may be that such answers attempt to make explicit. The former sense corresponds to that use of the term *grammar* in which a grammar may be a grammar book or a grammatical treatise (*Priscian's grammar, the Port Royal grammar*), and a rule would accordingly be a statement contained therein. The latter sense corresponds to that use of the term *grammar* in which one might still speak of Latin grammar and its rules even if Priscian's grammar had never been written and Rome had produced not a single grammarian. This difference can be made clear in all kinds of ways. For instance, the question 'In which language is Priscian's grammar written?' is a different question from 'Which language is Priscian's grammar a grammar of?', even though the answer to both may be 'Latin'. But it makes no more sense to ask 'In which language is the grammar Priscian wrote about written?' than to ask 'In which language does one play chess?' Similarly, it would make no difference to the game of cricket as played if the laws were all renumbered; but it would make a difference to the text of the MCC's *Laws of Cricket*.

One of the problems associated with the games analogy is that it tends to encourage a conflation between rules and rule-formulations. For the term *rule* is commonly used to cover both. Even Wittgenstein occasionally falls into this trap. He says, for instance, that there is no rule 'for how high one throws the ball in tennis' (PU:68). But this is simply wrong. The rule is that the server can throw the ball to any height. What Wittgenstein presumably means here is that the official I.T.F. list contains no rule-formulation of the form 'The server may not throw the ball more than *x* feet high' (which is correct). Nevertheless, the point is fully covered by Rule 7.

Such distinctions, however, are criss-crossed by others, which may likewise be formulated as accounts of various senses of the terms *grammar, rule*, etc. No one who has read either Saussure or Wittgenstein would leap in where angels fear to tread and attempt to give a simple lexicographical sketch-map for these and related words. It remains nevertheless true that any such sketch-map, however inadequate in other respects, would have to show *some* topographical connection between rules and grammars, and between grammars and games. Wittgenstein does not even question the connection:

> No one will deny that studying the nature of the rules of games must be useful for the study of grammatical rules, since it is beyond doubt there is some sort of similarity between them. (PG:187)

Wittgenstein is particularly concerned to clarify the connection between knowing the rules and being able to give the rules (i.e. to produce appropriate rule-formulations).

What's the sign of someone's understanding a game? Must he be able to recite the rules? Isn't it also a criterion that he can play the game, i.e. that he does in fact play it, even if he's baffled when asked for the rules? Is it only by being told the rules that the game is learnt and not also simply by watching it being played? Of course a man will often say to himself while watching "oh, so that's the rule"; and he might perhaps write down the rules as he observes them; but there's certainly such a thing as learning the game without explicit rules. (PG:62)

Wittgenstein evidently intends this analogy to carry over to language. Knowing the language is not a question of being able to explain what the rules are if asked (although that might be one way of exhibiting one's knowledge). Knowing the language is also exhibited in speaking it. But how does 'grammar' fit into this account? Wittgenstein continues: 'The grammar of a language isn't recorded and doesn't come into existence until the language has already been spoken by human beings for a *long* time.' (PG:62–3) Does this mean that the grammar does not exist until recorded? Evidently not, since otherwise many languages would have no grammars; and Wittgenstein does not recognise a special class of 'grammarless' languages. What is it, then, that doesn't come into existence until 'a *long* time' after the language was first spoken, and which we (or Wittgenstein) may still call its *grammar*? Presumably, its codification. And this answer seems to be confirmed by the immediately following comment: 'Similarly, primitive games are played without their rules being codified, and even without a single rule being formulated.' (PG:63)

Unfortunately, Wittgenstein now seems to have boxed himself into a corner which the wily pugilist of the *Cours* carefully avoids. How does any grammar (*langue*) come into existence? The question of the origin of language had been a toughly weathered philological chestnut for generations. Wittgenstein may not have been well acquainted with the relevant European literature, but Saussure certainly was. That particular *topos* had a cultural pedigree which included such famous names as Condillac, Rousseau, Herder and Monboddo. During Saussure's own lifetime the Société de linguistique of Paris had banned all papers on the subject, because it was perceived to be a quite unanswerable *and irrelevant* question. Yet Wittgenstein, pleading *sancta simplicitas*, raises it again in the early 1930s.

How can a game like chess be played before a single rule has been formulated? How can a language be spoken before it has any grammar? It is tempting to offer Wittgenstein a hand to help him out of the pit which he has apparently dug for himself. For example, why not say: 'The grammar is what we *subsequently* recognise, after codification, as having operated — and still operating — in these and these episodes of speech/play'? But Saussure, for one, would have recoiled in horror from any such helping hand. It is an apologia which conjures up the spectacle of speakers in ninth-century Paris, whose ghosts tell us in spectral confidence: 'Now we are safe in heaven, we can see that on earth we were speaking French. But at the time, as God is our witness, we thought we were speaking Latin.' Heaven is mostly an invention of theorists. And linguistic heavens are entirely inventions of linguistic theorists. If Saussure had any apostolic message for linguists it was: 'Heaven is now.'

The question is not a question about whether we call this or that piece of *parole* 'Latin' or 'French'. Or about what it was called, or might have been called, at the time. The question is whether anyone can be speaking French if there is no such thing as French grammar; or, to adapt Wittgenstein, 'without a single French rule being formulated'. If taken seriously at all, the question must be granted to be substantive. Otherwise it deflates with a bang at the first nominalist puncture.

Saussure's short answer (see p. 82) is that the only substantive grammatical question is psychological; although it is not a psychological question about speakers' attitudes or beliefs, any more than the question of whether they are playing by the rules of chess is a question about their attitudes or beliefs. Wittgenstein's short answer is more subtle; or, if we take a less generous view, more evasive.

Wittgenstein's short answer is to say of grammar what Voltaire said of God: had it not existed, it would have been necessary to invent it. This is simply a way of parrying both the ontological and the aetiological question in one effortless move. But its very effortlessness invites dissatisfaction. Has Wittgenstein really shown (as distinct from asserting) that playing is *eo ipso* proof of understanding the game? Or that the game can be learnt without leaning on the crutch of explicit rules?

We can imagine the case of a lad who has picked up the game of cricket simply as a spectator. No one has told him what the rules are, and he has never inquired. He never listens to or takes part in talk about cricket. He is invited to play, and acquits himself impeccably in many matches. He is invited to umpire, and acquits himself no less impeccably in that capacity too. Let us suppose that he even graduates to umpiring in first-class matches without taking the usual tests (which would, unfortunately, require him to articulate his knowledge of cricket verbally). Eventually he is appointed to the panel of Test Match umpires. All this is because of his apparently flawless grasp of the game. Miraculously, he never gives a wrong decision: batsmen, bowlers and fielders are alike convinced that his judgement is invariably correct. This is not because, by good fortune, he is never presented with difficult decisions. On the contrary, he has countless difficult decisions; but the television cameras, the experts, the players themselves, always in the end corroborate his verdict. As an umpire at the highest level, he is the infallible Mr Finger. Who better to cite as an example to illustrate Wittgenstein's claim that assiduous observation and practice suffice to acquire an understanding of the game without any need for explicit rules?

At the peak of his umpiring career, however, some wretched sports journalist on the *Daily Squeal* tumbles to the fact that Mr Finger cannot give even the most rudimentary account of the l.b.w. law, and whips up a great controversy in the media. How can this man umpire at Lord's when he does not know the basic rules of the game? The trouble is not that Mr Finger is tongue-tied, lacks the relevant vocabulary, or cannot match his answers to the questions about cricket which quiz-masters shoot at him. The trouble is that he *has no answer* to questions about the l.b.w. law, even though he has given thousands of apparently correct l.b.w. decisions over the years. It emerges that he has never realised, in spite of all his experience, that what matters is whether or not the ball would have hit the wicket. This thought has never entered his head in all his summers on the square. Nor does he now, when the law is read out to him, agree that 'that was really always the basis of his judgement, even though he may have failed to realise it at the time'. Furthermore, he does not intend to start taking what the laws say into consideration at this late stage in his cricketing life. Arrogantly, he challenges the MCC to find a better umpire among those who supposedly 'know the rules'. What will Wittgenstein say about this unrepentant but superbly efficient Mr Finger?

There are indications in Wittgenstein's writings that he was uncomfortably aware of the problem. He attempts to finesse it at one point by distinguishing between 'criteria' and 'symptoms'.

> To the question "How do you know that so-and-so is the case?", we sometimes answer by giving '*criteria*' and sometimes by giving '*symptoms*'. If medical science calls angina an inflammation caused by a particular bacillus, and we ask in a particular case "why do you say this man has got angina?" then the answer "I have found the bacillus so-and-so in his blood" gives us the criterion, or what we may call the defining criterion of angina. If on the other hand the answer was, "His throat is inflamed", this might give us a symptom of angina. I call "symptom" a phenomenon of which experience has taught us that it coincided, in some way or other, with the phenomenon which is our defining criterion. Then to say "A man has angina if this bacillus is found in him" is a tautology or it is a loose way of stating the definition of "angina". But to say, "A man has angina whenever he has an inflamed throat" is to make a hypothesis.
>
> In practice, if you were asked which phenomenon is the defining criterion and which is a symptom, you would in most cases be unable to answer this question except by making an arbitrary decision *ad hoc*. It may be practical to define a word by taking one phenomenon as the defining criterion, but we shall easily be persuaded to define the word by means of what, according to our first use, was a symptom. Doctors will use names of diseases without ever deciding which phenomena are to be taken as criteria and which as symptoms; and this need not be a deplorable lack of clarity. (BB:24–5)

For a doctor, as Wittgenstein says, it need not matter. But *mutatis mutandis* it is precisely what does appear to matter in the life of a cricket umpire. And it is also precisely at this point that the analogy between language and games with publicly codified rules begins to break down. The MCC's *Laws* are essential to cricket in a way in which Priscian's grammar (or any other) is not essential to Latin. When Mr Finger rejects the official l.b.w. law he proclaims his own incompetence as an umpire, whereas someone who has never heard of Priscian's rule of adjectival agreement is not *eo ipso* incompetent in Latin. Sadly, Mr Finger, for all his umpiring expertise, does not understand the game of cricket. The miserable hack on the *Daily Squeal* was right. At best, Mr Finger may perhaps understand a very similar game (snicket), whose rules are related to the rules of cricket in such a way that whenever a batsman is out in snicket he would also have been out in cricket. Or perhaps snicket has no rules at all; that is, no codifiable practice in the sense in which cricket is codified. For whatever else codification may be, or grammar too, it can hardly be just an open-ended inventory of particular cases, which good judges extend as they see fit. The 'rules' would indeed then be 'arbitrary', but in a quite different sense.

* * *

An important feature of the parallel between the rules of games and rules of grammar is that they serve no purpose external to the system to which they belong. Wittgenstein points out that this is part of what is meant by the term *game*. He asks 'Are the rules of chess arbitrary?' and answers his own question as follows:

> Imagine that it turned out that only chess entertained and satisfied people. Then the rules aren't arbitrary if the purpose of the game is to be achieved.
>
> "The rules of a game are arbitrary" means: the concept 'game' is not defined by the effect the game is supposed to have on us. (PG:192)

But a set of rules is not *eo ipso* autonomous in this respect. Wittgenstein contrasts both language and chess with cookery.

> Why don't I call cookery rules arbitrary, and why am I tempted to call the rules of grammar arbitrary? Because I think of the concept "cookery" as defined by the end of cookery, and I don't think of the concept "language" as defined by the end of language. You cook badly if you are guided in your cooking by rules other than the right ones; but if you follow other rules than those of chess you are playing another game; and if you follow grammatical rules other than such and such ones, that does not mean you say something wrong, no, you are speaking of something else. (PG:184–5)

Wittgenstein's comparison with cookery is perhaps not entirely happy, inasmuch as the rules of a recipe ('Take two eggs, . . . etc.') are externally determined in two ways. First, they have to be ordered: certain steps have to precede others, and cannot be arbitrarily reversed. Similarly in chess certain moves have to precede others. But in the case of grammar it is not immediately clear in what sense, if any, rules are ordered. However, the point about cookery is that any ordering in the procedures laid down by a recipe is determined entirely by their physical effects. One cannot blanch the almonds before the water has boiled, and so on. Whereas in games the ordering itself may be arbitrary. It might have been a rule of chess that all the pawns had to be moved before the knight could be moved. This has no counterpart in cookery.

Second, the rules of a recipe are externally determined in the sense that even if it were possible to carry out the steps in any desired order (as in the mixing of certain ingredients), nevertheless the purpose of the rules is ultimately to produce a given end-product (a cake, an omelette) and not merely to regulate the conduct of the cook.

It is this second mode of external determination, rather than the first, which is important in Wittgenstein's conception of the autonomy of grammar. As he puts it: 'Grammar is not accountable to any reality. It is grammatical rules that determine meaning (constitute it) and so they themselves are not answerable to any meaning and to that extent are arbitrary.' (PG:184) Even more specifically: 'The connection between "language and reality" is made by definitions of words, and these belong to grammar, so that language remains self-contained and autonomous.' (PG:97)

It is this lack of 'accountability to reality' which for Saussure distinguishes language from all other major social institutions. In these other cases social behaviour and its attendant conventions are geared to conditions and objectives which are imposed by the realities of the external world. Saussure denies that this is so in the case of language.

> Other human institutions — customs, laws, etc. — are all based in varying degrees on natural connexions between things. They exhibit a necessary conformity between ends and means. Even the fashion which determines the way we dress is not entirely arbitrary. It cannot depart beyond a certain point from requirements dictated by the human

body. A language, on the contrary, is in no way limited in its choice of means. For there is nothing at all to prevent the association of any idea whatsoever with any sequence of sounds whatsoever. (CLG:110)

* * *

It might perhaps be objected that in their insistence on the autonomy of grammar both Saussure and Wittgenstein are pressing the analogy between languages and games too far. Games are games, so the objection might run, precisely because they have no connection with the rest of social life or intellectual activity. They afford us a welcome opportunity to opt out of everyday routines and relax; and the self-contained, insulated character which games have is essential to this function. That is why their rules are arbitrary and are not 'accountable to reality'. Whereas with language it is exactly the opposite. Languages are not set apart from the rest of social life. Linguistic activity is all-pervasive. Linguistic communication is essential to keep the daily social mechanism in working order. So although it may be true that whether adjectives follow nouns or nouns follow adjectives in one sense makes no more difference than whether the king moves one square at a time or two squares at a time, nevertheless it is pushing the comparison beyond all reasonable limits to claim that English is no more 'accountable to reality' than chess. That would be not merely an exaggeration but a profoundly misleading conclusion. After all, what the king on the chessboard can or cannot do bears no relation to what a real king can or cannot do. Whereas the linguistic moves we make with the English word *king* do bear an important relation to what a real king can or cannot do: and it could hardly be otherwise, because an important reason for having a word *king* is to be able to talk about what real kings do. Whereas it is no part of the reason for having a king in chess to be able to reflect or reconstruct the activities of real kings.

How might this objector be answered? Saussure's reply would be to make three points. First, the argument puts the cart before the horse. Of course there are real kings, and speakers of English use the word *king* to talk about them: but that is not what 'justifies' the word *king*. *Unicorn* is just as good an English word as *king*; but reality offers us no unicorns to provide a parallel justification. 'Having the word' is prior to 'having the thing' if we want to explain what we talk about. Anyone, for example, can enjoy sitting in the sun; but there are languages in which it is impossible to speak of *sitting in the sun*, even though there may be words for *sit* and *sun* (CLG:161). It is grammar which determines what can be said; not the physical possibilities available in the world in which we live.

Second, this is not a mere matter of peculiar quirks of lexicon or idiomatic expression: it applies generally to the broad divisions imposed by grammar.

> Take the distinctions between the various parts of speech. On what is the classification of words into nouns, adjectives, etc. based? Is it on some purely logical principle of an extra-linguistic nature, applied to grammar from outside like lines of longitude and latitude on the earth's globe? Or does it correspond to something which belongs within, and is determined by the language system? In other words, is it a synchronic reality? (CLG:152)

Needless to say, the traditional 'definitions' of the parts of speech lend support to the view that these distinctions correspond to features of external reality. Nouns are said to be names of things or persons, adjectives names of properties or qualities, and so on. But to take the possibility of constructing 'external' definitions of this rough-and-ready kind as a demonstration that grammar is based on divisions already provided by Nature would again be to put the cart before the horse. For grammar allows us to say things which simply cut across any 'natural' divisions supposedly reflected by the parts of speech. For example, in French one can say *ces gants sont bon marché* ('these gloves are good value'). Now is *bon marché* ('good value') an adjective here? If not, what is it?

> For *bon marché* does not behave like a normal French adjective: it is invariable, never precedes its noun, and so on. Furthermore, it consists of two words. What the parts of speech provide is a classification of individual words: so how can a group of two words belong to one or other of the parts of speech? Yet if we split it up into two words, and say *bon* ('good') is an adjective, whereas *marché* ('value') is a noun, we have not accounted for the single expression *bon marché* ('good value'). (CLG:152-3)

The fact is that French grammar allows us to use *bon marché* here in place of a single adjective: but this has no 'external' justification in terms of the realities of gloves, prices, or anything else.

Third, no one denies that a language is integral to the life of a community, or that it serves a multitude of purposes which games could not conceivably serve. A language has connections with institutions and occupations of every kind, and supplies verbal equipment for them. From information about a community's vocabulary one could construct a far better picture of the life of the community than from information about the games it plays. For language is constantly adapting to changing circumstances.

> It is sometimes claimed that it is absolutely impossible to separate all these questions from the study of language itself. That is a view which is associated especially with the insistence that science should study 'Realia'. Just as a plant has its internal structure modified by outside factors, such as soil, climate, etc., in the same way does not grammatical structure depend constantly on external factors of linguistic change? (CLG:41–2)

Certainly it does, argues Saussure: but that is no more reason for denying the autonomy of grammatical structure than for claiming that in order to understand the rules of chess one has to know that the game originated in Persia. In short, the argument rests upon a conflation of 'external' with 'internal' linguistics. Grammar does not belong to external linguistics; and no external approach allows us to grasp the nature of grammatical facts.

Wittgenstein's reply will run along different but parallel lines. In effect, he elaborates Saussure's distinction between external and internal linguistics into a regress argument by asking the objector how it is possible to 'justify' grammar externally.

> The rules of grammar cannot be justified by shewing that their application makes a representation agree with reality. For this justification would itself have to describe what is represented. And if something can be said in the justification and is permitted by its grammar — why shouldn't it also be permitted by the grammar that I am trying to justify? Why shouldn't both forms of expression have the same freedom? And how could what the one says restrict what

the other can say? (PG:186–7)

Here the tables are turned on any demand for a justification of grammar by pointing out that any justification will need its own grammar, which will in turn stand in need of justification, and so on. But if at some point the regress is finally halted because we reach a grammar which 'justifies itself', does not that show that the original demand for justification was misguided? And if the regress can never be halted, does not that likewise show that the quest for justification is vain? We are mistaken if we think that we can somehow get outside language in order to explain language.

> What is spoken can only be explained in language, and so in this sense language itself cannot be explained.
> Language must speak for itself. (PG:40)

Wittgenstein goes to greater lengths than Saussure to attack the notion that what grammar allows us to say is already fixed by a reality outside language.

> One is tempted to justify rules of grammar by sentences like "But there are really four primary colours". And if we say that the rules of grammar are arbitrary, that is directed against the possibility of this justification. Yet can't it after all be said that the grammar of colour words characterizes the world as it actually is? (PG:185–6)

Wittgenstein's move here is to allow that it can indeed be said that 'there are really four primary colours', but to argue that the last thing one can build on that is a proof that our colour vocabulary is therefore 'correct'. 'May I not really look in vain for a fifth primary colour? (And if looking is possible, then finding is conceivable.)' (PG:186)

Wittgenstein, however, leaves himself more vulnerable than Saussure on the question of autonomy because of his constant appeal to very simple 'language game' examples. For instance, the builder's language of PU:2 is described in terms which appear to play straight into the hands of an objector who holds that languages, unlike games, have a structure which is in the end determined by external purposes. The builder's language is clearly designed to function in the context of a particular constructional enterprise. Its minimal vocabulary only 'works' because it answers very exactly to an external reality: namely, that blocks, slabs, pillars and beams are the only four types of building material the job requires. Any larger vocabulary would be superfluous and any smaller vocabulary inadequate: but the superfluity and the inadequacy are alike determined by physical factors relating to the building. So although it is undeniable that the individual signs are arbitrary (in the sense that any other four Saussurean *signifiants* would do just as well), how can it be claimed that the grammar as a whole is arbitrary (i.e. autonomous)?

Wittgenstein did not perhaps take as much care over elucidating this aspect of the autonomy of grammar as is needed. For it might reasonably be said that his own demonstration of the non-autonomy of rules of cookery could be applied also to the builder's language. The end-product is not a cake but a building; and the building cannot be put together in any old order, for purely physical reasons. So where is the difference?

Some of Wittgenstein's other illustrative examples seem to run headlong into a similar problem: for example, his comparison of grammar with a keyboard:

> let us compare grammar with a system of buttons, a keyboard which I can use to direct a man or a machine by pressing different combinations of keys. What corresponds in this case to the grammar of language?
>
> It is easy to construct such a keyboard, for giving different "commands" to the machine. Let's look at a very simple one: it consists of two keys, the one marked "go" and the other "come". Now one might think it must obviously be a rule of the grammar that the two keys shouldn't be depressed simultaneously (that would give rise to a contradiction). But what does happen if we press them both at the same time? Am I assuming that this has an effect? Or that it has no effect? In each case I can designate the effect, or the absence of an effect, as the point and sense of the simultaneous depression of both keys. (PG:188–9)

Here it seems that the button grammar is autonomous only in the sense that it allows the possibility of pressing both buttons simultaneously, even though this results in a problematic instruction. One can, doubtless, resolve the problem in ways consistent with the given grammar. For instance, one could treat the message 'Go: come' as meaning 'Do either.' Or one could treat the two as cancelling each other out, and meaning 'Stay put.' The button grammar is autonomous inasmuch as it does not resolve the problem for you, and is 'indifferent' to which solution is adopted. But that does not prove that the structure of the keyboard as a whole is not 'accountable to reality'. On the contrary, if it were not, the 'problem' would not arise, and *ex hypothesi* the keyboard would not have been constructed in the first place. The only lesson that emerges is that it might have been better to construct a keyboard in which the 'go' button and the 'come' button could not be depressed simultaneously. Then there would have been no 'slack' in the grammar.

The easy way out here would be to exculpate Wittgenstein by saying that it is unfair to press his particular examples too hard, or expect them to yield insights they were not designed to give. Analogising must come to an end somewhere. But this way out may be not only too easy, but actually do less than justice to Wittgenstein. For it is tantamount to declaring a non-contest between Wittgenstein and his hypothetical adversary over the autonomy question.

Wittgenstein's problem is that there is a tension between two possible interpretations of his rather cryptic remarks about the autonomy of grammar. On the weaker interpretation all he is saying is that an instrument must exist, and must have a specific structure, before any musician can play it, or compose music for it. In that sense, the instrument itself pre-sets limits to what the musician can do, while leaving open such questions as what is to count as a tune, whether the tune has been correctly played, and so on. Thus to say 'language must speak for itself' is like saying 'the instrument must play for itself'; and to deny that grammar is accountable to reality is like denying that an instrument is accountable to acoustics. It would be quite absurd, for example, to try to 'justify' the octave intervals of a piano keyboard by reference to the corresponding ratios of cycles per second (even though that might be relevant to settling arguments about whether or not a particular piano were in tune). Likewise it would be absurd to suppose that the grammar of the pianoforte was the same as the grammar of the guitar.

At other times, however, the claim seems to be a far more controversial one. According to this stronger interpretation, the autonomy of grammar is not simply a question of every linguistic system being independent and self-contained. Rather, the thesis is that grammar is the internal organisation which imposes

82

constraints on what can meaningfully be said; and to this extent grammar has already taken the external world into account, just as in the construction of a musical instrument account has already been taken of the possible range of notes to be played. Precisely for that reason there has to be an inner coherence to the structure in both cases.

> If we had grammar set out in the form of a book, it wouldn't be a series of chapters side by side, it would have quite a different structure. And it is here, if I am right, that we would have to see the difference between phenomenological and non-phenomenological. There would be, say, a chapter about colours, setting out the rules for the use of colour-words; but there would be nothing comparable in what the grammar had to say about the words "not", "or", etc. (the "logical constants").
>
> It would, for instance, be a consequence of the rules, that these latter words unlike the colour words were usable in every proposition; and the generality belonging to this "every" would be not the kind that is discovered by experience, but the generality of a supreme rule of the game admitting of no appeal. (PG:215)

This is much more akin to saying that it is the structure of the musical instrument which ultimately determines the criteria of harmony. If so, not even the most imaginative of composers will be free, beyond a certain point, to invent; because some sounds and sound sequences which it is physically possible to produce are simply a musical abuse of the instrument. And this is not a question of anyone's tolerance of experimental music. The iconoclast who writes pieces for the piano which are played by banging a saucepan on the keys is not a profound musical revolutionary, but either a joker or a mental case. It is not that using a saucepan demands a new technique with its own refinements, to which we are not yet accustomed. The claim is that someone who bangs the keyboard with a saucepan, even in accordance with a score designed expressly for that purpose, is not playing the piano.

* * *

Wittgenstein never tells us where grammar comes from.

Saussure at least tries to. The *Cours* speaks of 'a grammatical system' which every member of the linguistic community possesses, and which has been acquired in each individual case 'through the practice of speech' (CLG:30). But the grammar of a sentence cannot be derived simply from hearing it spoken. Otherwise, learning foreign languages would be a trivially simple matter. Experience shows us this is not the case. If we hear a Chinese sentence but know no Chinese, then all we hear, as Wittgenstein puts it, is 'a mere series of sounds' (PG:152). The difference between 'a mere series of sounds' and a meaningful utterance is grammar.

Grammar, according to Saussure, is a spontaneous product of the human mind, which springs from 'two different forms of mental activity' (CLG:170). One is the analysis of events into temporal sequences. This yields a classification of units on the basis of their relative positions in a sequence. The other form of mental activity is comparison on the basis of similarities. This yields a classification of units on the basis of likeness of sound and likeness of meaning. The combined product of these two forms of mental activity is a systematisation of our experience of speech. In the first instance, we experience speech passively as a 'succession of sounds uttered by others'. The dual process of systematisation extracts from this material sets of recurrent units, which are related to one another in two dimensions: syntagmatically, as units which can be arranged in linear sequences, and associatively, as units which belong to 'associative series' linked by similarities of form and meaning. This process of systematisation is going on all the time at an unconscious level in the human mind as new speech experience is assimilated: Saussure speaks of this constant analysis and re-analysis as the 'continual activity' of language.

Grammatical enquiry, according to Saussure, does not attempt to discover exactly how this mental systematisation is carried out or its results stored and utilised. Nevertheless, the ideal grammatical description will be a description of the end-product.

One may say that the sum total of deliberate, systematic classifications set up by a grammarian studying a given linguistic state a-historically must coincide with the sum total of associations, conscious or unconscious, operative in speech. These are the associations which establish in the mind the various word families, flexional paradigms, formative elements, stems, suffixes, endings, etc. (CLG:189)

Grammar is thus in no sense accessible to direct observation. A grammatical description is simply a hypothesis. Furthermore, it is a hypothesis which, in its more abstract details, cannot hope to be confirmed: 'one can never be sure whether the awareness of speakers of the language always goes as far as the grammarians' analyses.' (CLG:190) In the end, therefore, grammar for Saussure remains a mystery, since its organisation is never fully revealed in the actual operations of speech.

Here again cracks begin to show in the analogy with games. What would one think of the chess expert who said: 'Of course, we can't be sure of *all* the rules'? (And did not mean that perhaps in ancient Persia the game had rules we did not know about.)

8

Variation and Change

The idea that the structure of a linguistic system is comparable to the structure of a game, although potentially enlightening in many respects, also brings in its train a certain number of problems, which Saussure and Wittgenstein attempt to deal with in various ways. Arguably the most serious of these problems is that of determinacy, which subsumes a variety of particular questions concerning variation and change. Someone playing a game of chess knows that the game has fixed rules, that the pieces have determined roles in the game, and plays accordingly. But is this true of someone speaking English?

English, it might be argued, is subject to endless variation. Not only is Brown's English never exactly the same as Smith's English, and the English of one area or stratum of society never exactly the same as another's, but the whole system is undergoing incessant change over time and open to unpredictable innovation. So where is there any determinacy of the kind which is characteristic of chess?

Saussure meets the problem of linguistic change head on and deals with it ruthlessly, whereas Wittgenstein simply does not allow it to arise. Saussure could hardly afford to do otherwise, since the study of linguistic change had been the mainstay of nineteenth-century linguistics. Wittgenstein on the other hand could afford to say nothing, since philosophy had never bothered about it. Both strategies are predictable, given the historical context of their respective disciplines.

Saussure's draconian solution is to posit an absolute distinction between synchronic facts and diachronic facts, to reject the systematicity of linguistic evolution, and to deny that linguistic systems as such ever change. The illusion that they do change, according to Saussure, is simply the product of historical perspective, which confounds *faits de langue* with *faits de parole*. In opting for this uncompromising stand, Saussure took an influential and unprecedented step in the history of linguistic theory.

Time and again throughout the *Cours* warnings are repeated and illustrations given to emphasise the confusions which ensue from failing to distinguish between the synchronic and diachronic domains. To the former belong all 'static facts' and to the latter all 'evolutionary facts'. There is no overlap.

> The consequences of the radical difference between facts of evolution and static facts is that all notions pertinent to the former and all notions pertinent to the latter are mutually irreducible . . . No synchronic phenomenon has anything in common with any diachronic phenomenon. (CLG:129)

The methodological consequences of this for Saussure are of paramount importance: 'The contrast between the two points of view — synchronic and diachronic — is absolute and admits no compromise.' (CLG:119) Failure to grasp this can only lead to a misunderstanding of the mechanisms of linguistic change.

> Since changes are never made to the system as a whole, but only to its individual elements, they must be studied independently of the system. It is true that every change has a repercussion on the system. But initially only one point is affected. The change is unrelated to the internal consequences which may follow for the system as a whole. This difference in nature between chronological succession and simultaneous coexistence, between facts affecting parts and facts affecting the whole, makes it impossible to include both as subject matter of one and the same science. (CLG:124)

The lengths to which Saussure is prepared to go to defend this theoretical position are, by the lights of his day, remarkable. Two whole chapters of the *Cours* (CLG:221–37) are devoted to arguing that so-called 'analogical changes' are not changes at all (in spite of being unanimously treated as changes by Saussure's contemporaries). A standard textbook example, the disappearance of the nominative case in Old French, is denied to be an example of grammatical evolution (CLG:132). All this is in support of the thesis that 'the language system as such is never directly altered. It is in itself unchangeable.' (CLG:121)

Wittgenstein, understandably, does not feel the need to carry the fight into the enemy camp in quite the way that Saussure does. He implicitly dismisses linguistic change in a few brief remarks. At one point in the *Philosophische Grammatik* a hypothetical objector worries over the fact that if we are to have a rule 'there must at least be a regularity through time' in its use. Otherwise we might be interpreting it differently at different times; and then it would be unclear how one would know how it was to be interpreted in any given case. Wittgenstein replies brusquely: 'Well, how does one know *anyway*? Explanations of signs come to an end somewhere.' (PG:94) The problem of 'regularity through time' could hardly get shorter shrift.

Elsewhere he takes a position very similar to Saussure's, distinguishing between two uses of the word *chess*, depending on whether or not it makes sense to envisage the rules as changing. He speaks of:

> the double use of the word "chess" to mean at one time the totality of the currently valid chess rules, and at another time the game invented in Persia by N. N. which developed in such and such a way. In one case it is nonsensical to talk of a development of the rules of chess and in another not. (PG:238)

This corresponds exactly to Saussure's distinction between synchronic and diachronic perspectives. From one point of view, that of the current language-user, it is nonsense to talk of the rules of English changing, but from another point of view, that of the historian, it is not nonsensical. The important matter for Saussure, as for Wittgenstein, is not to confuse these points of view.

Saussure's reply to linguists who claim that language never stands still is to make two points. First, there are periods of time in the history of a language during which the changes which accrue are minimal (CLG:142). Hence it is not a misrepresentation to treat these periods as linguistic 'states' (*états de langue*). Second, in any case nothing prevents us from taking a chronological cross-cut at any point in time and describing the 'state' thus revealed (CLG:124–5). Wittgenstein makes a very similar point about the painting of a picture.

If we look at the actual use of a word, what we see is something constantly fluctuating.

In our investigations we set over against this fluctuation something more fixed, just as one paints a stationary picture of the constantly altering face of the landscape. (PG:77)

* * *

The problem of determinacy also arises on another front, where it engages Wittgenstein more overtly than Saussure. Granted that there is a valid perspective from which rules do not change, nevertheless do we have anything in the case of language which corresponds to the chess player's assurance of knowing precisely and incontrovertibly what the rule is? Does the word *knight* have a meaning which is fixed in the sense that the knight's move in chess is fixed?

Confronted with this problem, Wittgenstein often gives the impression of hopping from one foot to the other and hoping it will go away. For example:

> We are able to use the word "plant" in a way that gives rise to no misunderstanding, yet countless borderline cases can be constructed in which no one has yet decided whether something still falls under the concept 'plant'. Does this mean that the meaning of the word "plant" in all other cases is infected by uncertainty, so that it might be said we use the word without understanding it? Would a definition which bounded this concept on several sides make the meaning of the word clearer to us in *all* sentences? Would we understand better all the sentences in which it occurs? (PG:117)

Perhaps not, one might reply; but it is nevertheless an awkward admission for someone to make who is proposing to construe the meaning of a word as 'its use in the language'. For if analogous uncertainties arose in the case of the chess player and the knight's move, then it would begin to look as if *either* the player did not after all know the rule *or* that there was after all no fixed rule to be known. Would there be any more point in having a word whose 'use in the language' was uncertain than a chess piece whose legitimate moves on the board were undecided?

We can observe a similar shuffle when Wittgenstein deals with the Sherlock Holmes mystery of the disappearing chair:

> I say "There is a chair". What if I go up to it, meaning to fetch it, and it suddenly disappears from sight? — "So it wasn't a chair, but some kind of illusion". — But in a few moments we see it again and are able to touch it and so on. — "So the chair was there after all and its disappearance was some kind of illusion". — But suppose after a time it disappears again — or seems to disappear. What are we to say now? Have you rules ready for such cases — rules saying whether one may use the word "chair" to include this kind of thing? But do we miss them when we use the word "chair"; and are we to say that we do not really attach any meaning to this word, because we are not equipped with rules for every possible application of it? (PU:80)

'Doubtless not' is again the answer to Wittgenstein's rhetorical question. Holmes has once again demonstrated that stupid Watson has jumped to the wrong conclusion. But it is the rhetorical question itself which sidesteps the crucial issue. Disappearing chairs do not demonstrate the meaninglessness of the word *chair* any more than dubious plants prove the meaninglessness of the word *plant*. But that very fact points up a *dis*analogy with the rules of chess. The rule of the knight's move *does* cover all possible positions on the chess board. Whereas in the case of language it is up to the user to *decide* what to call the dubious plant or the disappearing chair. This has no parallel in the game of chess because the game of chess is not open-ended in the way language is. Perhaps Watson had a point after all.

Wittgenstein does not deny that there are games in which we make up the rules as we go along, or even alter them as we go along (PU:83). But this admission hardly helps. For to the extent that language resembles games of that kind it is typically *un*like playing chess. The whole point of the chess analogy is that the rules *do* determine in advance all the possible moves, and that the grammar of the game is *not* decided by individual players as the spirit moves them. Games which are not like chess in this respect, although they may have every right to count as games, simply do not supply the right model for explicating the institutional character of language, its regularity and its autonomy. Once we come to games where play is an improvised free-for-all, there is not only no guarantee that different players are not playing by different rules but no clear way of making good the claim that there are any rules at all.

This leads directly to a question which adopting the 'games' perspective constantly brings up in one form or other: how much variation is compatible with the notion that players are playing the same game? Again, it is Saussure who takes the logic of the games analogy unhesitatingly to its conclusion while Wittgenstein hedges. Theoretically, for Saussure, a difference of a single phoneme or a single sign suffices to distinguish two separate sign systems. And he does not shrink from the conclusion that what are commonly called 'languages' (English, French, Latin, etc.) are not in his sense synchronic sign systems, but conglomerates of historically related dialects and sub-dialects. It is at the dialectal and sub-dialectal levels that the linguist will hope to identify the real 'idiosynchronic' systems which speakers actually use at any given time (CLG:128).

Sometimes Wittgenstein too seems to be sympathetic to this view. He considers the case of someone who says: 'I can assure you I feel the visual image to be two inches behind the bridge of my nose.'

> We don't say that the man who tells us he feels the visual image two inches behind the bridge of his nose is telling a lie or talking nonsense. But we say that we don't understand the meaning of such a phrase. It combines well-known words, but combines them in a way we don't yet understand. The grammar of this phrase has yet to be explained to us. (BB:10)

The implication here seems to be, clearly, that this man is speaking a different subvariety of English from ours: for if his grammar were the same as ours, then presumably we *should* understand what he is saying. Nevertheless, we recognise the words he uses and doubtless some familiar combinatorial patterns. So in Saussurean terms the case seems to be that of someone using a different idiosynchronic system, but one which is closely related historically to our own. (The games analogy here would be that of a variant of chess in which we fail to understand an episode of play because we have not grasped, say, that in this idiosynchronic variant the king cannot be put in check when standing on his own square.)

What Wittgenstein does not discuss, however, is the

complementary question of whether we understand this individual if he says, for example, 'I am finding it rather difficult to focus my eyes on you.' This may sound like a perfectly unproblematic sentence of our own variety of English; but since we have now been alerted to the fact that his grammar is not the same as ours, the last thing we can take for granted is that we know what he means. Perhaps he means that the visual image keeps shifting to one and a half inches behind his left ear.

Elsewhere, however, Wittgenstein claims that we do understand the sentence 'I eat a chair', even though we were not taught the meaning of the expression *eating a chair* (BB:21). In this case, presumably, our grammar is deemed to do the job for us. But what is unclear is whether we do in fact understand 'I eat a chair' any better than 'I feel the visual image two inches behind the bridge of my nose.' More surprisingly still, he thinks we understand the assertion that ten thousand million souls fit into a cubic centimetre (RFM:135), and asks why nevertheless we do not say that. His rather curious answer is not that it is false but: 'Because it is of no use. Because, while it does conjure up a picture, the picture is one with which we cannot go on to do anything.' (RFM:135) He also concedes:

> It might be found practical to call a certain state of decay in a tooth, not accompanied by what we commonly call toothache, "unconscious toothache" and to use in such a case the expression that we have toothache, but don't know it . . . Now is it wrong in this sense to say that I have toothache but don't know it? (BB:22–3)

His again somewhat curious answer is: 'There is nothing wrong about it, as it is just a new terminology and can at any time be retranslated into ordinary language.' (BB:23) But how there can be any question of retranslation into ordinary language if *ex hypothesi* the expression *unconscious toothache* has become established usage it is difficult to see.

The awkwardness is particularly acute in view of Wittgenstein's keenness to remind us

> that a word hasn't got a meaning given to it, as it were, by a power independent of us, so that there could be a kind of scientific investigation into what the word *really* means. A word has the meaning someone has given to it. (BB:28)

All the more reason, one would have thought, for dispensing with any appeal to retranslation into ordinary language as a way of justifying meanings.

The difficulty for Wittgenstein seems to be his wish to cling to the notion that grammatical rules autonomously determine what can be (sensibly) said and what cannot be; yet at the same time allow the common-sense provision that deliberate linguistic innovation may take place, linguistic usage be allowed to change, and sensible new uses be found for combinations of words previously regarded as nonsensical. The unsolved problem is whether any reconciliation of these conflicting requirements is ultimately possible within the scope afforded by the games analogy. It is indeed possible to introduce changes in the Laws of Cricket; but incoherent to insist on trying to introduce them during the course of play.

Nor does Saussure deal any more convincingly than Wittgenstein with the problem of semantic change. This lacuna was already noted in 1916 by the editors of the *Cours* (CLG:33fn.). Given Saussure's categorical denial of the systematicity of linguistic change, the reason for his reticence is not difficult to see. He would need an account which parallels his account of sound change. In other words, he needs to maintain the thesis that change is accidental and fragmentary, never affecting signs as such, but only their realisation in *parole*. This is relatively easy to maintain in the case of *signifiants*, since a *signifiant* is decomposable into meaningless phonemic units, and the phenomena of change can be located at that level of structure. The trouble is that in the case of *signifiés* there is no parallel level of structure. In consequence, whenever Saussure has to deal with an example of linguistic change which cannot be explained away on phonetic grounds, we find him struggling. He is driven, as noted above, to the rather desperate expedient of claiming that the 'new' forms which appear are simply realisations of potential forms which already existed in the language, but had never been used (CLG:221ff.). When it comes to explaining the semantic aspects of changes in morphology and syntax, he has to make the even more extraordinary claim that at one stroke the semantic value of a formal distinction can simply be 'lost' for no apparent reason (CLG:132). When it comes to discussing how a verb which originally meant 'to kill' changes in meaning to 'drown', he has no explanation to offer at all (CLG:109). He nevertheless insists that all linguistic innovation originates in *parole*. This is evidently another case of a change in the l.b.w. law being negotiated on the field of play; but, even more surprisingly, by players whom Saussure has already declared unauthorised to do so. At such points, presumably, the game must come to a standstill. Communication breaks down, and must somehow be repaired: a new system of rules must be brought in to replace the system just discarded.

9

Communication

Neither Saussure nor Wittgenstein questions the lay assumption that language is primarily a form of communication and that languages are to be viewed as communication systems. From a 'games' perspective, no other assumption is admissible. Wittgenstein's language games are all communication games. Saussure's archetypal speech act is one of dialogic communication. In terms of the chess analogy, communication is a matter of the players' appropriate responses to each other's moves in accordance with the rules of the game. At first sight nothing could be less problematic. Yet it is here, with this apparently quite harmless assimilation, that difficulties begin to emerge for both Saussure and Wittgenstein which cannot lightly be brushed aside.

The games analogy is seen as appropriate because, as Wittgenstein puts it, 'A game, a language, a rule is an institution.' (RFM:334) This institutionality, moreover, is reflected in recurrent social activity. Saussure would have agreed with Wittgenstein's remark that: 'In order to describe the phenomenon of language, one must describe a practice, not something that happens once, *no matter of what kind*.' (RFM:335) Anyone who is thus far committed to the games analogy is automatically led to construe linguistic communication as the counterpart of the activity of play in which the players engage. Wittgenstein goes so far as to say 'the concept of language *is contained in* the concept of communication' (PG:193). One might equally say that the concept 'game' is contained in the concept 'play'. It is difficult, having gone thus far, now to back out of a purely contractualist account of linguistic communication: for this is the obvious alternative to a surrogationalist account. But a purely contractualist account is not easily given (Harris 1980:120ff.).

Within a surrogational framework of the Aristotelian kind (see Chapter 4) verbal communication posed no theoretical problem. For if we are willing to take for granted Aristotle's assumption that the human race shares a common set of 'mental affections', of which words are simply signs, then a word automatically means the same for any two or more individuals acquainted with its proper use. Consequently, verbal communication between one individual and another is assured, provided they are familiar with the same words; just as they may unhesitatingly engage in commercial transactions provided they are using the same currency. Aristotle's words have the same meaning as Hermias', which is why Hermias can understand Aristotle's lectures. Hermias' drachma has the same value as Aristotle's drachma, which is why Aristotle accepts payment in coin from Hermias. Communicational difficulties arise only in the absence of a common language, just as commercial difficulties may arise in the absence of a common currency.

However, the comforting reassurance that shared words guarantee communication sags as soon as the Aristotelian assumption that all human beings have a common fund of perceptual experience and concepts is called in question. If each individual's private mental world is always in certain respects different from that of any other individual, there is no cast-iron guarantee that the same words are similarly understood by those who use them. And if, furthermore, as Locke and his followers assumed, the mind of each individual is initially a *tabula rasa*, its eventual contents determined solely by the sense impressions received during the course of that individual's lifetime, it is difficult not to conclude that every human mind must be unique. Words become at best a very hazardous and imperfect method of communication, being mediated by the unknown and unpredictable stock of ideas which have accumulated in the minds of different individuals. Hence Locke speaks of 'the imperfection of words' and concludes that understanding takes place only when 'the sound I make by the organs of speech excites in another man's mind who hears it the idea I apply to it in mine when I speak it' (Locke 1706:3.3.3).

More explicitly still:

> To make words serviceable to the end of Communication, it is necessary that they excite, in the Hearer, exactly the same *Idea*, they stand for in the mind of the Speaker. Without

this, Men fill one another's Heads with noise and sounds; but convey not thereby their Thoughts, and lay not before one another their Ideas, which is the end of discourse and Language. (1706:3.9.6)

Saussure's model of verbal communication is unmistakably cast in the Lockean mould. This is evident from his account of the 'speech circuit' (*circuit de la parole*), which runs as follows. Two interlocutors, *A* and *B*, are imagined to be talking to each other.

The starting point of the circuit is in the brain of one individual, for instance *A*, where facts of consciousness which we shall call concepts are associated with representations of linguistic signs or sound patterns by means of which they may be expressed. Let us suppose that a given concept triggers in the brain a corresponding sound pattern. This is an entirely *psychological* phenomenon, followed in turn by a *physiological* process: the brain transmits to the organs of phonation an impulse corresponding to the pattern. Then sound waves are sent from *A*'s mouth to *B*'s ear: a purely *physical* process. Next, the circuit continues in *B* in the opposite order: from ear to brain, the physiological transmission of the sound pattern; in the brain, the psychological association of this pattern with the corresponding concept. If *B* speaks in turn, this new act will pursue — from his brain to *A*'s — exactly the same course as the first, passing through the same successive phases . . . (CLG:28)

From the above account it is evident (i) that verbal communication is for Saussure a telementational process, its objective being the transference of a thought from *A*'s mind to *B*'s, (ii) that the criterion of successful communication is the reception by *B* of the thought which *A* transmitted through the mechanisms of the speech circuit, and (iii) that, apart from the sound waves, no part of this is external to the speakers, for the situational context plays no role in the communicational process. These are also features of Locke's account. Consequently Saussure appears to inherit automatically all Locke's problems. How can such a model offer any assurance that communication ever takes place? Any attempt at verbal clarification between *A* and *B* will be subject to doubts of exactly the same kind as in the case of the utterance which required clarification in the first place. Saussure's speech circuit thus emerges as a closed circuit of communicational problematics, from which there is no obvious way to break out.

Locke has also been taken as typical of the philosophers to whom Wittgenstein's arguments against the possibility of a 'private language' are addressed (Hacker 1986:255ff.). Locke's insistence that no one can apply words 'immediately, to anything else but the ideas that he himself hath' (1706:3.2.2) sounds remarkably reminiscent of Wittgenstein's hypothetical adversary who insists that the word *toothache* refers, at least in the first instance, to an absolutely private experience. 'The essential thing about private experience is really not that each person possesses his own exemplar, but that nobody knows whether other people also have *this* or something else.' (PU:272) According to Locke, this will apply not just to our ideas of 'toothache' or 'red', but to all our ideas and the corresponding words.

Memory plays a crucial role in Locke's account of language, and an even more crucial one in Saussure's. Locke is not greatly concerned with the problem of remembering how to combine words.

> The function of memory for Locke is to provide the filing cabinet for the speaker's exemplars, and to produce the correct exemplar for each word as the speaker has need of it. Thus memory ensures that one uses the same sign for the same idea. Wittgenstein's private linguist envisages a similar procedure. (Hacker 1986:257)

But Saussure might well have pointed out both to Locke and to Wittgenstein's private linguist that this is not enough, and that our memory must hold in store not only the total inventory of individual signs but also 'all the various types of syntagma, of every kind and length.' (CLG:179) For communication would also break down if we were always forgetting whether the subject preceded the object or vice versa.

Thus far Saussure's position on communication can be seen as ultra-Lockean, and contrasting sharply with the later Wittgenstein's anti-Lockean stance. Wittgenstein is evidently sceptical of the whole telementational model:

we are so much accustomed to communication through language, in conversation, that it looks to us as if the whole point of communication lay in this: someone else grasps the sense of my words — which is something mental: he as it were takes it into his own mind. If he then does something further with it as well, that is no part of the immediate purpose of language. (PU:363)

The concept of 'communication' looms ever larger in Wittgenstein's own intellectual odyssey. The basic difference between the philosophy of language we find in the *Tractatus* and the philosophy of language we find in the *Philosophische Untersuchungen* might perhaps be put as follows: in the former work language is seen as a means of depicting reality, whereas in the latter work language is seen as a means of communication. That difference is already apparent from the very first example which Wittgenstein uses to criticise the nomenclaturist view of language presented by Augustine (see Chapter 2).

Augustine does not speak of there being any difference between kinds of word. If you describe the learning of language in this way you are, I believe, thinking primarily of nouns like "table", "chair", "bread", and of people's names, and only secondarily of the names of certain actions and properties; and of the remaining kinds of word as something that will take care of itself.

Now think of the following use of language: I send someone shopping. I give him a slip marked "five red apples". He takes the slip to the shopkeeper, who opens the drawer marked "apples"; then he looks up the word "red" in a table and find a colour sample opposite it; then he says the series of cardinal numbers — I assume that he knows them by heart — up to the word "five" and for each number he takes an apple of the same colour as the sample out of the drawer. — It is in this and similar ways that one operates with words. — "But how does he know where and how he is to look up the word 'red' and what he is to do with the word 'five'?" — Well, I assume that he *acts* as I have described. Explanations come to an end somewhere. — But what is the meaning of the word "five"? — No such thing was in question here, only how the word "five" is used. (PU:1)

Here we see straight away how the appeal to 'communication' is used to cut through the tangle of nomenclaturist assumptions about language. The example is deliberately unrealistic. The shopping expedition would not in real life be conducted in this manner. No greengrocer keeps apples in drawers labelled 'apples', or consults colour charts. Nevertheless, we do not refuse to recognise the outcome as communicationally valid. The point is not whether greengrocers do or do not go through such routines when customers come in with shopping lists; but that the logic of everyday communication does not demand what the nomenclaturist assumes — namely, that every word must have something for which it stands, and this 'something' is its meaning.

This line of attack is immediately pressed home with the example of the builder's language (PU:2). Here the undermining of the Augustinian thesis about language is both comprehensive and subtle. Wittgenstein plays the nomenclaturist at his own game. For the builder's language could convincingly be described in purely nomenclaturist terms. The words *block, pillar, slab* and *beam* will be identified by the nomenclaturist as names of four different types of object; and this account fits the case. The point Wittgenstein is making is that it only fits because it relates to a communication situation which does not place any more complex demands on the language.

At first sight it looks as if the problems built in to Saussure's speech circuit do not arise for Wittgenstein's account of communication. There simply is no difficulty about whether or not the builder's assistant understands the meaning of the word *slab*. It is not a question of whether the concept of a slab in the builder's mind matches the concept of a slab in the assistant's mind. For the Wittgensteinian criteria of successful communication do not appeal to hidden mental events at all. Provided the assistant fetches a slab when the builder calls 'Slab!', a beam when the builder calls 'Beam!', and so on, then their communication *is* successful. Nothing further can be demanded, and the Lockean puzzle has vanished into thin air.

Someone unconvinced by this Wittgensteinian conjuring trick might say: 'But surely the assistant still has to *recognise* the right building materials to bring in response to each call. How does he do that?' Wittgenstein concedes to this objection:

We could imagine what happened in such a case to be this: In B's mind the word called out brought up an image of a column, say; the training had, as we should say, established this association. B takes up that building stone which conforms to his image. (BB:89)

However plausible such a story sounds, argues Wittgenstein, there are other possible explanations:

> was this *necessarily* what happened? If the training could bring it about that the idea or image — automatically — arose in B's mind, why shouldn't it bring about B's *actions* without the intervention of an image? This would only come to a slight variation of the associative mechanism. Bear in mind that the image which is brought up by the word is not arrived at by a rational process (but if it is, this only pushes our argument further back), but that this case is strictly comparable with that of a mechanism in which a button is pressed and an indicator plate appears. In fact this sort of mechanism can be used instead of that of association.
>
> Mental images of colours, shapes, sounds, etc. etc., which play a role in communication by means of language we put in the same category with patches of colour actually seen, sounds heard. (BB:89)

Whether this response disposes of the objection is a different question. More immediately relevant to our present purposes is that, when thus spelled out, Wittgenstein's communicational scenario begins to look suspiciously like Saussure's on at least the following counts:

(a) When the assistant heard the word, *something* went on in his head, the exact nature of which we do not know, which was causally efficacious in sorting out which of the types of building material he was to fetch.

(b) This was not necessarily a rational process.

(c) It did not necessarily involve, nor was it necessarily accompanied by, a pictorial image.

(d) It was probably automatic, a kind of triggering process.

The main difference between Wittgenstein and Saussure now seems to hinge on the fact that Saussure speaks of a 'concept' having been triggered; whereas Wittgenstein suggests that it might be B's 'actions' which are triggered directly.

Anyone who feels that Saussure's account here is preferable might be inclined to defend it along the following lines. Saussure's term 'concept' is deliberately vague, and Saussure never attempts to give it a more precise delineation. So nothing much hangs on calling *what* is triggered a 'concept' except this: it allows for a mental buffer, as it were, between the hearer's auditory identification of the word uttered and the inception of those motor programmes which constitute taking appropriate action. What, in general, is wrong with any model which allows words directly to trigger hearers' actions is that a human being then becomes a linguistic automaton. And that makes nonsense of our daily linguistic experience. The world we live in is not one in which instructions are automatically executed, requests granted, and so on. The theoretical role played by Saussure's 'concepts' is precisely to allow for the possibility of understanding what is said, but *without* acting on it. Unless Wittgenstein wishes to deny that possibility (which seems unlikely), then any Wittgensteinian criticism of Saussure's speech circuit must in the end boil down to a terminological quibble. It will mean no more than decomposing Saussure's pairs of 'concepts' and 'sound patterns' into something more sophisticated — a move already anticipated in the *Cours* (CLG:28–9).

But now it begins to look disconcertingly as if we are back to square one. The conjuring trick which made Locke's puzzle vanish was accomplished simply by sweeping it under the communicational carpet. It was made to appear that the overt procedures of ordering and fetching slabs, beams, etc., because carried out visibly, in full theoretical daylight, were inherently less mysterious than occult processes in the heads of the interlocutors. ('Clearly, he's brought a slab: you can see it for yourself.')

Seeing for yourself is the final court of appeal incessantly invoked by professional conjurors. There is never anything up the magician's sleeve. Wittgenstein takes the stage as a philosophical conjuror who denounces his rivals' use of curtains, mirrors and trick lighting; but then announces 'Genuine self-levitation is performed like this' and remains rooted to the spot.

* * *

Bringing communication out into the open and banishing

mumbo-jumbo about recondite mental events may well be salutary and sweep away much obfuscation; but it does not instantly dispel every communicational enigma. Particularly if one still claims, as Wittgenstein does, that 'If language is to be a means of communication there must be agreement not only in definitions but also (queer as this may sound) in judgments.' (PU:242) For this claim immediately resurrects something very similar to Locke's puzzle. What is this mysterious linguistic 'agreement'? How is it arrived at? How do we know it is being observed?

From the way Wittgenstein phrases it, it sounds as if we are expected to take the 'agreement in definitions' as a reasonably uncontroversial requirement, but to be somewhat taken aback by the concomitant 'agreement in judgements'. A recent careful exegesis of the passage in question confirms this reading:

> Obviously agreement in definitions is necessary; for if two people disagreed about how to explain the words they use, then what the one meant by an utterance would not be what the other understood by it, and to this extent communication would have broken down. But Wittgenstein adds the surprising requirement that there also be agreement in judgements. (Baker and Hacker 1985:258–9)

If this interpretation of what is 'obvious' and what is 'surprising' is right, however, it seems that one must be careful not to exaggerate Wittgenstein's disagreement with Locke. For notwithstanding all the cold water poured on Lockean 'ideas', it would appear that Locke's basic explanatory framework for communication remains intact. Instead of demanding that A and B share covert 'ideas', the demand is now that they share overt 'explanations'. But it is by no means clear that Locke would wish to disagree. This new demand, indeed, captures the essence of his proposals concerning the establishment of a 'scientific' language. The need, claims Locke, is for overt consensual regulation of the definition of terms. What is odd about Locke's position here is also odd about Wittgenstein's: namely, taking it for granted that *that* is the *sine qua non*.

'Communication' is one of those meretriciously perspicuous concepts: everything can be made to seem obvious, but very little is. It seemed obvious to Locke that communication requires agreement in ideas. It seemed obvious to Saussure that communication requires agreement in signs. It seemed obvious to Wittgenstein that communication requires agreement in definitions. But none of this is obvious. Nor is it even obvious that we should be much further forward if any of these requirements were in principle correct. The disservice which the games analogy does to our understanding of communication here is to make what is not at all obvious appear to be so.

If, for example, we see two people playing chess we assume (failing evidence to the contrary) that behind this lies an agreement about the rules. Analogously, we are led to assume when we see two people engaged in conversation that behind this lies a comparable agreement about the words. There may be room for dispute concerning exactly what this agreement about words consists in (as Locke's account, Saussure's account and Wittgenstein's account between them amply attest) but that there must be, somewhere and somehow, such an agreement seems 'obvious' once the parallel between chess and language is accepted. Otherwise, indeed, that parallel would be awry from the very start. For people do not just sit down and play chess without any rules.

Descriptive problems, it thus appears, may arise at the stage when we try to specify the terms of the linguistic agreement. But the analogy itself has already bypassed the question of whether there is such an agreement. Consequently, any possible difficulties over discovering what the agreement is in a given case are put down in advance to the multiple hazards which beset all empirical investigation of human behaviour; and the source of the trouble is never traced, nor traceable, to the initial 'agreement' assumption itself. Wittgenstein occasionally worries away at this theoretical sore spot, but cannot afford to worry too much, since he is committed just as much as Saussure to the thesis that language is systematic. (How could that be unless languages, like games, had their rules which the speakers/players agreed to?) Saussure also worries away at it, but again cannot afford to worry too much, since he is committed *qua* linguist to the thesis that linguistic systems are describable.

Rubbing away at theoretical sore spots is in any case discouraged by a desire for symmetry between descriptions of communication and explanations of communication. For example, when we look at the builder's language of PU:2 an understandable inclination is to describe this in terms of an agreement between the builder and his assistant. Must they not *agree* that 'Block!' is the call for a block, and so on? How else would the system work? But one 'else' might be simply that the builder and his assistant have been independently trained to act thus. (Wittgenstein's initial presentation of this language in PU:2 invites this interpretation: the assistant 'brings the stone which he has learnt to bring at such-and-such a call', but nowhere are we told that the builder taught him to do so.) As soon as we spot this, the notion of 'agreement' immediately begins to look problematic. What kind of agreement do I have with my neighbour which rests merely on our independent acceptance of living under a specifiable set of local by-laws? What kind of agreement do I have with my interlocutor which rests merely on our independent acceptance of the *Oxford English Dictionary* as authoritative for English usage?

The games analogy is ideal for laying all such doubts to rest. Surely I cannot question whether I am really playing chess with this woman, even though I have never met her before in my life. Her moves, her reactions, her response to my Ruy Lopez opening, her whole demeanour, all confirm my belief that we agree, and know we agree, and know that all spectators agree that we know we agree, that we are playing chess. Nor, surely, can I question whether I am really speaking English with this man, even though I do not know him, and he has never asked me the way to the railway station before. The sounds he utters, the look of enquiry on his face, his response to my tentative first sentence, all confirm my belief that we agree, and know we agree, and know that all the bystanders ready to proffer their own advice, should mine be found wanting, agree that we are speaking English. Would not all this be a miracle unless there really *were* such an agreement?

Nevertheless, there is a world of difference between producing the 'agreement' story as a *description* of what the builder and his assistant do, and producing the 'agreement' story as an *explanation* of what the builder and his assistant do. It is like the difference between saying that the Communists and the Social Democrats agreed in not opposing the bill, and saying that the Communists and the Social Democrats agreed not to oppose the bill. Unfortunately, this basic difference tends to get obliterated in examples like the builder's language, because of the stipulation that the words used for purposes of the building enterprise constitute their *complete* language. So how could the only two participants *agree* to act thus-and-so other than *in* acting thus-and-so? What form of prior verbal or non-verbal communication could serve to articulate such an agreement?

Suppose we take seriously the following ensemble of propositions: (i) that the four words which the builder and his assistant use constitute their complete language; (ii) that the builder and his assistant do communicate by means of this system; and (iii) that, as Wittgenstein maintains, linguistic communication requires agreement in definitions. What are the possibilities here for construing 'agreement in definitions' between the builder and his assistant?

The corresponding problem for Saussure, we may note, would be the question of determining what exactly the common system of signs is which the builder and his assistant use. How do we construe their 'agreement in signs', the shared matching of *signifiants* with *signifiés* which presumably underlies the successful *parole* on which the building operation depends?

Clearly, there can be no question of verbal definitions of the type: 'Let's define *block* as "prepared rectangular unit of hewn stone or wood . . . etc." ' For *ex hypothesi* the builder's language is too impoverished a system to cater for such definitions. But nothing prevents us from imagining that the builder and his assistant worked out their arrangement in some such way as follows. The builder uttered the word 'Block!', pointed to the pile of blocks, and then in dumb show went through the motions of fetching a block from the pile. Then he uttered the word 'Slab!', pointed to the pile of slabs, and pantomimed fetching a slab. And so on. Then he held a trial, which consisted of uttering the word 'Block!' and motioning the assistant to go and fetch one. The assistant did so, and the builder smiled, accepted the block, and showed every sign of being pleased with the result. But how did the assistant recognise that he had done the right thing in the trial? Wittgenstein himself provides us with an answer: 'The common behaviour of mankind is the system of reference by means of which we interpret an unknown language.' (PU:206)

Let us, then, grant that in some such fashion, by means of pointing and dumb show, the builder and his assistant have managed to set up their system. In order to achieve this, they have not needed to go outside the elements of the system itself, other than in utilising their recognition of certain features of 'the common behaviour of mankind'. But they have not used any prior verbal system in order to initiate this one. It is a system they have built up from the inside. Given all this, the question which interests us now is: what does their 'agreement in definitions' consist in? The corresponding Saussurean question would be:

what does their sharing of a common sign system, their 'agreement in signs', consist in?

One answer might be: it consists simply in their common acceptance of the correlational patterns on which the whole regular procedure of recurrent calling and fetching rests. But there is something very odd about this as an explication of 'agreement in definitions'. When we watch a dog on the beach repeatedly rushing after and retrieving pieces of branch and driftwood thrown into the waves precisely for that purpose by the dog's owner, we do not say of this mutually co-operative pair, 'Ah, yes. Of course, they agree in definitions. Otherwise it could not possibly work.' And even if, curiously, we did say this of the dog's fetch-the-stick game, it is difficult to see how to cash the notion of definitional 'agreement' between dog and owner except as residing in the systematicity of their co-operation (in which case we have explained nothing, but merely given a bizarre re-description of what is going on), or else in terms of the shared expectations of the participants. But the moment we make *that* move we are into the obscure realm of mental processes, both human and canine.

Another answer might be: the agreement between builder and assistant consists in the recognition by each that both are using the same set of correlations for purposes of the calling and fetching operation. But the trouble with that answer is that the assumption might simply be wrong. Doubtless we shall never know as long as everything proceeds smoothly and there are no hitches in the building operation. But there could be. For example, perhaps the builder, with the remains of a lunchtime sandwich in his mouth, begins the afternoon's proceedings by uttering something which sounds like 'Black!'. The assistant makes no move, because *black* is not a word in his vocabulary; at which the builder shows evident signs of annoyance, to his assistant's great surprise. Or perhaps a few slabs have got into the pile of beams; so that on one occasion when the builder calls 'Beam!' he is brought a slab. This is because the assistant thought the operative correlation was between words and piles of materials, not between words and types of item. In Saussurean terms, this would show that builder and assistant were *not* associating the same concepts (*signifiés*) with the same sound patterns (*signifiants*).

What are we to say of such hitches? Has communication broken down? This is presumably what we must say if we accept the general thesis that without agreement in definitions (or signs), what one person means by an utterance is not the same as what another understands by it. But then, presumably, there had never been any communication at all between builder and assistant, even though the constant misunderstandings had never previously shown up. They may have thought they agreed in definitions; but they were mistaken. They may have thought they were using the same sign system; but they were not. It simply took a long time for them to discover that they were playing by different rules; hence not playing the same game.

Wittgenstein, unlike Saussure, explores various loopholes which might possibly afford ways of wriggling out of such an unwelcome conclusion. He points out, for example, that it is too much to expect rules to cover every conceivable eventuality. There is no rule, he (mistakenly) claims, for how high the server throws the ball in tennis: 'yet tennis is a game for all that and has rules too.' (PU:68) This is Wittgenstein playing his 'common sense' card. Another of the same suit is to claim that exceptions destroy everything if they become as frequent as 'normal' cases. The grocer would not weigh our lump of cheese on the scale and charge us according to its weight if lumps of cheese frequently increased or decreased in size for no apparent reason. *Mutatis mutandis* the same applies to words. 'It is only in normal cases that the use of a word is clearly prescribed.' (PU:142) Saussure, on the other hand, makes no provisos about 'normality'; and this may not be simply an oversight on his part.

The trouble with playing 'common sense' cards is that the suit is no longer trumps once we have declared that there *must* be agreement in definitions as a necessary condition of linguistic communication. In any case, it will not do to assimilate the hitch over 'Black!' to a case not covered by the rules. (In tennis the players *know* that there is no restriction on how high the ball may be thrown.) Nor will it do to treat as an abnormal case the possibility of a slab turning up in the beam pile: that is not the same as beams randomly turning into slabs on their way from the pile to the builder. This is not to deny the validity of Wittgenstein's general observations about gaps in the rules and normality conditions. Clearly, the builder's language will not work if the builder keeps eating sandwiches and never articulates anything clearly; nor in the face of frequent but unpredictable transmutations of beams into slabs, slabs into blocks, and so on. No system would work in such conditions. But that is not the point. The point is that when it emerges that the builder and his assistant did *not* after all 'agree in definitions', we are left with only a very limited set of options. One is to abandon the claim that the builder and his assistant were communicating. Another is to abandon the claim that agreement in definitions is necessary for communication. A third is to try to fudge some compromise; for instance, to say that before the hitch they did indeed communicate because in those cases their agreement was sufficiently close to deal successfully with the situation, but that they failed to communicate in the controversial cases because their agreement was not one hundred per cent.

The Saussurean predicament is on all fours with this. Either the account of the speech circuit has to be revised to accommodate cases in which linguistic communication is successful *even though* the speaker's concept does not match the hearer's, or else the case of the builder and his assistant is expelled from linguistics and relegated to whatever branch of semiology may deal with communication across different sign systems.

Whichever of the options is selected, three conclusions emerge. First, the appeal to 'agreement in definitions' or 'agreement in signs' is doing no explanatory work whatsoever. For either communication, if it takes place, takes place *in spite* of the lack of agreement; or else the agreement extends only to cases which turn out, in practice, to be trouble-free. Second, the problem is foisted upon us by the games analogy. The trouble is that the analogy does not fit. There simply is no counterpart here to the rules of chess, and it is misguided to insist that somewhere there must be, under pain of conceding that the verbal interaction between builder and assistant is not a form of verbal communication. Third, a Wittgensteinian analysis of the case is in no better shape than a Saussurean analysis. Both face exactly parallel problems. 'Agreement in definitions' is the Wittgensteinian translation of Saussure's identity of *signifiants* and *signifiés*.

* * *

What now of Wittgenstein's 'surprising' requirement that linguistic communication *also* demands agreement in judgements? It turns out not to be surprising at all. For if 'agreement in definitions' is doing as little useful work as it appears to be, something more concrete and pragmatic is surely required. But what is this 'agreement in judgements'?

> What 'agreement in judgements' means must be inter-
> personal consensus about the truth and falsity of a large body
> of empirical propositions. (Baker and Hacker 1985:259)

If so, this is unfortunate for our analysis of the builder's language, where questions about what is true and what is false *prima facie* do not arise. It is doubly unfortunate if we construe *truth* and *falsity* as being just ordinary words like any others. For this threatens to generate an altogether new and intractable problem as to why just these two words should occupy some kind of privileged position in the vocabulary; and in particular why they should hold any lien on our human rights to linguistic communication.

Truth, it might be suggested, is a special case of appropriateness; rather than appropriateness a special case of truth. And armed with this suggestion, we might propose a less narrow interpretation of Wittgenstein's 'agreement in judgements'. Perhaps all we need look for is some indication that, for example, when the builder calls 'Block!' and the assistant fetches a block, both judge this to be an appropriate outcome, and recognise each other as so judging. On what could such judgements be based, and how would they be recognised? Here it is tempting to fall back once again on 'the common behaviour of mankind'. If the builder recognises what the assistant has done as appropriate, he accepts the block, does not throw it aside, glare, howl with rage, clout the assistant's ear, and so on. Nor does the assistant expect such behaviour if he judges his bringing the item in question to be an appropriate response to the call 'Block!'. An account along these lines can doubtless be filled out with all the relevant details and qualifications so as to pass muster as a behavioural explication of 'appropriate-ness' and judgements thereof.

Let us for the moment suppose that we now have such an account all filled out. The first point that may strike us is this: that it renders any account of 'agreement in definitions' superfluous. More precisely, it brings us to realise that an 'agreement in judgements' between the builder and his assistant supersedes, or rather subsumes, their 'agreement in definitions'. To put it another way, there is little point in their agreeing in definitions (whatever that may amount to) unless in practice that can be translated into agreement in judgements. We might be encouraged in that conviction by the more general reflection that this squares with our everyday notion of 'communication'. Thus, for example, it will do the interior decorators Drip and Splash little good to agree on defining the word *green* as meaning 'the colour between blue and yellow in the spectrum' if every sample of paint which Drip calls 'green' Splash pronounces to be 'yellow', and every sample of paint which Spash calls 'green' Drip pronounces to be 'blue'. On that basis they would do better to join forces as lexicographers than as interior decorators.

If, on the other hand, Drip and Splash invariably agree about particular samples of green paint, it will make no difference at all to their interior decorating business if they cannot agree on a lexical paraphrase for the word *green*. In that case they would be well advised to stick to decorating and leave lexicography alone. *Mutatis mutandis* the same applies to the builder and his assistant, for whom in any case lexicography hardly offers a promising career.

For Saussure 'agreement in judgements' plays no comparable role; and it would be wrong to underestimate how radically, in consequence, his position differs from Wittgenstein's. Saussurean linguistics is 'segregationalist' in the sense that it assumes the possibility of a strict segregation between linguistic and non-linguistic phenomena within the universe of human activity. More prosaically, it assumes that human linguistic behaviour can be separated out from accompanying non-linguistic behaviour, and treated independently. Hence for Saussure linguistic analysis is a quite different enterprise from the analysis of the use of languages by individuals or communities. For Wittgenstein, on the other hand, language has no segregated existence; words are always embedded in a 'form of life' (PU:19). His hypothetical language games are inextricably integrated into purposeful human activities of some kind, as in the archetypal case of the builder and his assistant. Hence for Wittgenstein a description of the builder's language involves more than an exhaustive account of its verbal equipment, which is all a Saussurean linguist would feel obligated to give. This is the other part of the explanation (see Chapter 5) why Wittgenstein draws no rigorous distinction of the kind which Saussure draws between *langue* and *parole*. For Wittgenstein, we might say, play is the best part of the game.

From a Saussurean point of view, if the builder and his assistant agree in any given instance that the assistant has responded appropriately to the builder's call (e.g. by bringing a block in response to the call 'Block!'), that is merely a result of successful linguistic communication, not an integral part of it. On the contrary, successful linguistic communication might equally have resulted in disagreement. This is because for Saussure communication simply depends on whether, over the relevant segments of the speech circuit, speaker and hearer identify the same linguistic sign. In each case, communication is already complete — or has failed outright — before the assistant even sets off to fetch the required item. Linguistic communication, in brief, for Saussure is internal to the speech circuit itself, and does not in any way depend on practical consequences which ensue from speech.

One might attempt to summarise this important difference between Saussure and Wittgenstein by saying that for Wittgenstein the speech circuit is not complete until the assistant has fetched the block; whereas for Saussure that operation lies outside the speech circuit altogether. Hence both the importance of 'agreement in judgements' for Wittgenstein, and its irrelevance for Saussure.

One remarkable consequence of Saussure's position is that it would be theoretically possible, in Saussurean terms, for the builder and his assistant *never* to agree, even though both were using the same language, and there were no breakdown in communication. This is because for Saussure the linguistic sign is defined differentially: the relevant criteria are always contrastive criteria. The same principle applies both to the sound patterns and to the associated concepts, and it lies at the heart of the Saussurean concept of linguistic 'values'.

> If we say that these values correspond to certain concepts it must be understood that the concepts in question are purely differential. That is to say they are concepts defined not positively in terms of their content, but negatively by contrast with other items in the same system. What characterises each most exactly is being whatever the others are not. (CLG:162)

This insistence on the contrastive identity of linguistic signs is summed up in one of the most commonly quoted Saussurean epigrams: *In the language itself, there are only differences.* (CLG:166)

Because of this insistence on purely differential criteria, it is possible to envisage a case in which the builder and his assistant reach a total deadlock in the building operation, because the item the assistant brings never corresponds to what the builder wants.

This could arise if, for example, the various types of building material were distinguished one from another simply by combinations of relative size, relative weight, relative rigidity, relative porosity, and so on, and the 'distinctive semantic features' of the system were accordingly 'bigger versus smaller', 'heavier versus lighter', 'more rigid versus less rigid', etc. It would then be possible for the builder and his assistant to 'agree in definitions' of the terms to be used (*block*, *slab*, etc.) but never to agree on the application of a term to any single item in stock (because they take different views of what counts as big enough to be a 'bigger' object, heavy enough to be a 'heavier' object, etc.). The result is that the builder always rejects the assistant's 'block' because it is too small, but when a bigger 'block' is brought rejects that because it is too porous, and so on. How and why two sane individuals would ever devise such a Mad Hatter's classification is, needless to say, a puzzle: but language is not proof against lunacy.

Nor are Saussurean differential definitions proof against the lunacy of a language which is theoretically in order but unusable in practice because no two users have learnt the same pronunciation. Consequently, when A pronounces a word B cannot recognise it; this might happen even though A and B are using the same phonological system (i.e. there is an agreed set of 'phonological definitions', but wide individual differences in the phonetic realisations of the speech sounds). This would complement exactly the hypothetical case described in the preceding paragraph: a Mad Hatter's phonology to go with a Mad Hatter's semantics. (But it is worth noting *en passant* that the Mad Hatter phonology is not so far removed from the sanities of everyday linguistic experience as the Mad Hatter semantics seemed to be. It is, after all, not ludicrous to say that two people cannot read each other's handwriting, even though they are adhering to the same orthography, the same alphabet, and writing twentieth-century English.)

Spelling out the Mad Hatter's paradox is neither a mere *jeu d'esprit* nor a *reductio ad absurdum* of Saussurean linguistics (any more than the small child's comment on the spider that 'Its legs are ridiculous' was a criticism of the principle of natural selection) But it is true that if the builder and his assistant had *per impossibile* managed to combine a Mad Hatter phonology with a Mad Hatter semantics they would together have had a hard time of it building the Tower of Babel. The Tower of Babel myth lends itself to a quite straightforward Saussurean exegesis. Overnight, God scrambled one or more connections in the speech circuit. The next morning in the land of Shinar everybody was still apparently speaking the same common language as the night before. Unfortunately, however, the assistants could no longer understand what the builders were saying. God might have brought this about in several ways, for the Saussurean speech circuit is vulnerable to various types of communicational disjunction. To list these possible breakdown points is the simplest way of giving a full analysis of Saussure's concept of communication and its relationship to that of *parole*. There are seven such points in all:

(a) failure of connection between A's original concept and the appropriate sound pattern in A's brain;

(b) failure of connection between the sound pattern in A's brain and the appropriate motor programme involving A's organs of speech;

(c) failure internal to the motor programme itself;

(d) failure in the transmission of sound waves, due to external 'noise';

(e) failure in the auditory programme relaying sounds from B's ear to B's brain;

(f) failure in the identification of the sound pattern in B's brain;

(g) failure in the connection between sound pattern and concept in B's brain.

God could have chosen to effect a systematic disruption at any one of these seven points. A Mad Hatter phonology will produce a breakdown at (f), but nowhere else. A Mad Hatter semantics will produce no breakdown at all in the speech circuit as such. But it will be just as effective in halting progress in the construction of the Tower of Babel.

Wittgenstein discusses a case of Mad Hatter semantics when he imagines a community who sell wood by piling timber in heaps on the ground and charging for it according to the ground area covered by each pile. They justify this by saying: 'Of course, if you buy more timber, you must pay more.'

> How could I shew them that — as I should say — you don't really buy more wood if you buy a pile covering a bigger area? — I should, for instance, take a pile which was small

by their ideas and, by laying the logs around, change it into a 'big' one. This *might* convince them — but perhaps they would say: "Yes, now it's a *lot* of wood and costs more" — and that would be the end of the matter. (RFM:94)

The end of bargaining, certainly: but, *pace* Wittgenstein, only the beginning of the slippery slope of language. Wittgenstein closes the discussion thus:

We should presumably say in this case: they simply do not mean the same by "a lot of wood" and "a little wood" as we do; and they have a quite different system of payment from us. (RFM:94)

Saussure would doubtless have agreed about the payment. But from a Saussurean point of view it is by no means clear that 'their' English and 'our' English constitute different idiosynchronic systems. The story as Wittgenstein tells it is perfectly compatible with their signs *more, less, wood,* etc. having exactly the same semantics and syntagmatics as ours do. They simply value timber differently: but that does not mean they do not speak English.

How does Saussurean linguistics avoid the Mad Hatter's paradox? Simply by situating linguistic systems in time. This move fills the theoretical gap which Wittgenstein plugs by demanding 'agreement in judgements' between language-users. It comes to the same thing in the end. By situating *la langue* in time (that is to say, in the cultural history of a community) the theorist can take as given the prior establishment of correlations which are communicationally relevant to that community. There is never any questioning of these correlations because they have been handed down 'with the language'. They form the basis of the judgements about which there is — necessarily — agreement within the community; and without which there could be no common language.

*   *   *

The problem of communication, then, is to be solved by postulating a common language. The main difference between Saussure's and Wittgenstein's solutions seems to lie in what they include in this 'common language'. Saussure's *langue* is a public system of signs which provides all its users with an identical stock of private concepts and associated sound patterns. Wittgenstein more generously includes in his common language not only 'agreement in definitions' but also 'agreement in judgements', which seems at first sight to cover much more. Or does it?

'Agreement in judgements' will presumably have to extend to the auditory identification of words. This is an aspect of verbal communication which Wittgenstein, unlike Saussure, passes over in silence. But it is no less fundamental. As the hitch with 'Black!' indicates, it seems essential that the builder and his assistant should get the phonological parameters of their system sorted out. Unless this is somehow included under Wittgenstein's dual agreement, then his account of linguistic communication, as Saussure would doubtless have pointed out, must be judged seriously incomplete. Its incompleteness would be particularly striking in a system under which there is no room for checking: *ex hypothesi* the assistant cannot respond in cases of doubt by saying, 'Excuse me: did you say *block?*'

But let us give Wittgenstein the benefit of the doubt and extend his 'agreement in judgements' to cover this too. If so, it begins to look as if the builder and his assistant are now much more powerfully equipped by Wittgenstein for successful linguistic communication than they would be under the provisions of Saussure's *langue*. For that only guarantees identity of phonological structure, which in itself (as noted above) gives no assurance that a hearer will recognise a speaker's pronunciation of any given word.

It seems, then, that we shall need to break down the notion of 'agreement in judgements' according to the various kinds of judgement involved: phonetic judgements, judgements of size and shape, judgements of sequential ordering, correlational judgements, and so on. In this way we could attempt to specify in some detail exactly what 'agreement in judgements' is needed in order to operate this particular system of communication; that is, to underwrite the 'appropriateness reactions' of the builder and the assistant respectively to particular transactional episodes. An elaborate descriptive programme, but a feasible one; and defining in the end a much more powerful communicational instrument than Saussure's *langue*.

This will doubtless further encourage us in the belief that 'agreement in judgements' is really the crux of the matter. Provided *that* is assured, how can the builder and his assistant go wrong? But a little extra reflection may give us pause on two counts.

First, are we really any further forward than with 'agreement in definitions'? Is not this new, fully-fledged account of 'agreement in judgements' simply an elaborate way of dressing up the hollow truism that communication will be successful as long as, in practice, the calling-and-fetching operation continues smoothly. But whether it will, only time can tell. For it would defeat the whole purpose of the enterprise if the builder and his assistant had to plan each and every step in advance, checking that there were no stray slabs among the beams, no blocks with corners chipped off, no unforeseen difficulties of any kind. It makes nonsense of having a communication system if dress rehearsals are called for whenever it is brought into use. So to claim that agreement in judgements is a necessary condition of communication is to say no more than that any system will work, provided no *disagreement* arises over particular cases. But we knew that from the start.

A second qualm is much more disturbing. If the only proof of the communicational pudding is in the eating, what does it matter whether the builder and his assistant are actually using two different systems, provided that this does not affect their agreement in judgement over any particular case? (And this agreement, let us remind ourselves, is to be defined in overt behavioural terms: it is not a private seal of mental approval.) So if the builder and his assistant can somehow agree not to disagree over particular cases, however awkward, it hardly matters exactly where the boundaries of their system (or systems) are deemed to be drawn. An observer watching the operation might perhaps be tempted to pass such comments as 'The builder ought really not to have accepted that as a slab,' or 'The assistant ought really not to have accepted that grunt as the word *block*.' But if the builder and his assistant are so tolerant, such pedantry from outsiders can have no possible justification. As far as communication is concerned, it is what the builder and his assistant successfully *do* which defines what is permissible, not vice versa. But it would be exactly the opposite if they were playing chess.

To reach this conclusion is to see that the kind of activity in which the builder and his assistant are engaged is in the end fundamentally different from chess, however hard we try to stretch the analogy. There is no prior set of rules they have to conform to, because they are co-operating, not competing. They are free to use verbal signs in any way which will further that co-operation and get the job done. The example is revealing inasmuch as it highlights respects in which the general thesis that linguistic communication requires agreement in definitions and in judgements may be seriously misleading. It suggests, moreover, a preferable point of departure for any general enquiry into language: namely, that linguistic communication *is* the reaching of agreement by means of verbal signs in particular interactional episodes. Language starts there, and nowhere else: and that is also the point of departure for any sane alternative account to those which Saussure and Wittgenstein give us.

10

Language and Science

Saussure and Wittgenstein shared a deep dissatisfaction with the current academic practice of their own subjects. In each this is ascribable partly to what they considered its status to be *vis-à-vis* the natural sciences. They shared also a desire to place scholarly activity in their respective fields upon a sounder theoretical basis. Wittgenstein's misgivings concerning philosophy were manifest very early in his career; whereas Saussure's doubts concerning linguistics developed only gradually. Both, however, were convinced that most of their contemporaries and predecessors had failed to grasp the true object of enquiry in their own disciplines. Consequently, both felt that they were facing an uphill task, and both were outspoken and sweeping in their condemnations. Wittgenstein roundly declared that 'Most of the propositions and questions to be found in philosophical works are not false but nonsensical' (TLP:4.003), while Saussure claimed that he had difficulty in finding a single term in current linguistics that made any sense at all (letter to Meillet, 1894; de Mauro 1972:355). Each thought of himself as clarifying conceptual muddles which cluster round the topic of language; in one case the muddles introduced by linguists and in the other case the muddles introduced by philosophers.

The background to these complaints is the controversy about 'scientific' status which had been at issue since at least the 1850s, with academic subjects of every hue pressing their claims for recognition as 'sciences'. Not to be a science, not to adopt 'scientific methods', nor espouse 'scientific aims' was tantamount to lacking intellectual respectability in the universities of late nineteenth- and early twentieth century Europe. The claims made on behalf of both philosophy and linguistics in this regard are interesting.

A foremost champion of philosophy as 'science' was Wittgenstein's teacher, Russell, whose concern with the theme is evident in his Herbert Spencer lecture of 1914, 'On Scientific Method in Philosophy', and in his book *Our Knowledge of the External World as a Field for Scientific Method in Philosophy*, published in the same year. According to Russell, philosophy held the unique position of being the most general of the sciences. Like other sciences, however, it could advance hypotheses which were open to correction and thus could make 'successive approximations to the truth' (Russell 1914:109). With this Wittgenstein totally disagreed: 'Philosophy is not one of the natural sciences' (TLP:4.111). Nor, according to the *Tractatus*, is philosophy any other kind of science, since there are no genuine philosophical propositions. Philosophy, therefore, can tell us nothing about the world. The notion that it is the most general of the sciences is a fundamental misconception.

The same theme recurs as a *leitmotiv* in Wittgenstein's later work: 'Philosophy simply puts everything before us, and neither explains nor deduces anything.'(PU:126) Again: 'In philosophy we do not draw conclusions.' (PU:599) To the objection that since linguistic phenomena are, after all, facts of nature, anyone interested in understanding language ought to be interested 'not in grammar, but rather in that in nature which is the basis of grammar', Wittgenstein's reply is brief: 'we are not doing natural science.' (PU:p. 230) That remark would have been eminently appropriate as an epigraph to the chapter in Saussure's *Cours* devoted to 'The Object of Study'.

The claim that linguistics was a science had been advanced enthusiastically in the 1860s by Max Müller, who likened its methods to those of botany, geology and astronomy (Müller 1864:1). The title of the first of Müller's *Lectures on the Science of Language* at the Royal Institution in 1861 was quite explicit: 'The Science of Language one of the Physical Sciences'. Saussure rejected this categorisation because it was based upon the assumption that languages were organisms, having a natural pattern of growth, development and decay. He also rejected the notion that linguistics had proved its scientific status by establishing the operation of Indo-European 'sound laws' (as claimed by the Neogrammarian school), since he did not accept the phonetic developments in question as 'laws' (CLG:129ff.). Equally, he rejected the argument advanced by Hovelacque (1877:29ff.), on the basis of Broca's discoveries concerning the localisation of language in the brain, that linguistics was a physiological science (CLG:26–7). Saussure did, however, insist that linguistics was to be ranked among the human sciences, and specifically that it was a branch of the (hitherto unrealised) science of semiology.

This was to be 'a science *which studies the role of signs as part of social life*'. It would 'investigate the nature of signs and the laws governing them'. 'The laws which semiology will discover will be laws applicable in linguistics, and linguistics will thus be assigned to a clearly defined place in the field of human knowledge.' (CLG:33) By thus treating the study of *la langue* as a branch of a more general science, Saussure claimed to have 'for the first time succeeded in assigning linguistics its place among the sciences' (CLG:33–4).

The *Cours* and the *Tractatus* are in agreement as to what a science is, at least to the extent that a necessary condition is seen as being that a science must advance empirical propositions, and in that sense be descriptive. Precisely because philosophical propositions do not describe the world, even the most general aspects of the world, Wittgenstein denies to philosophy the status of a science. Even though 'All philosophy is a "critique of language" ' (TLP:4.0031), it is not a description of language. For Saussure, on the other hand, the first task of linguistics as a science is descriptive: it is 'to describe all known languages and record their history' (CLG:20). By the same token, although Saussure admits both philology and comparative philology as 'scientific' activities, he explicitly refuses this title to the efforts of grammarians to legislate on the subject of 'correct' usage (CLG:18–19). This is evidently because — and in so far as — the grammarians' approach to language is prescriptive, not descriptive. It is no function of the science of language, in Saussure's view, either to approve or to condemn features of ordinary usage. Likewise Wittgenstein disavows any interest in reforming everyday language, claiming that the propositions of everyday language are in perfect logical order just as they are (TLP:5.5563). This thesis is later reiterated in the *Philosophische Untersuchungen*:

> it is clear that every sentence in our language 'is in order as it is'. That is to say, we are not striving after an ideal, as if our ordinary vague sentences had not yet got a quite unexceptional sense, and a perfect language awaited construction by us. (PU:98)

123

The *Tractatus* is not concerned, as Russell mistakenly thought (TLP:x), with the problem of constructing a logically perfect language, but with analysing the conditions which all languages must fulfil. Saussure's science of language will also be concerned with conditions governing all languages; but these are empirical, not logical conditions.

The aims of linguistics will be:

(a) to describe all known languages and record their history. This involves tracing the history of language families and, as far as possible, reconstructing the parent languages of each family;

(b) to determine the forces operating permanently and universally in all languages, and to formulate general laws which account for all particular linguistic phenomena historically attested;

(c) to delimit and define linguistics itself. (CLG:20)

Saussure and Wittgenstein thus at first sight exhibit a clear complementarity of attitudes towards language and science. The 'division of labour' between linguistics and philosophy is plain. Linguistics for Saussure is the empirical study of the existential conditions of all languages (and hence a science). Philosophy for Wittgenstein is the conceptual analysis of the logical conditions of all languages (and hence not a science).

This complementarity, seemingly unproblematic on first inspection, conceals difficulties for both theorists. For the author of the *Tractatus*, 'the totality of genuine propositions constitutes the whole of "natural science" ' (Hacker 1986:23). Language on this view does not enable us to formulate ethical, aesthetic or metaphysical propositions; nor, worse still, propositions about the essence of language itself. These lie beyond the limits of language. And yet, in some sense, philosophy as practised in the *Tractatus* (a linguistically articulated text) does seem to yield a descriptive account of language; or at least of certain essential features of language. As Russell wryly observed, 'Mr Wittgenstein manages to say a good deal about what cannot be said' (TLP:xxi). How can this be? The puzzle turns up again in the *Philosophische Untersuchungen*, where philosophy is presented as concerned with description of the workings of language. 'There must not be anything hypothetical in our considerations. We must do away with all *explanation*, and description alone must take its place.'

(PU:109) Or again: 'Philosophy may in no way interfere with the actual use of language: it can in the end only describe it.' (PU:124) But then how is philosophy different from linguistics? And if linguistics is a science, why isn't philosophy? For both must be concerned with the use of words. 'Does it require philosophers to emerge from their armchairs and indulge in lexicography?' (Hacker 1986:161) The suggested answer is that such questions 'rest on a misunderstanding', that philosophy is not 'in competition with descriptive grammar', and that for Wittgenstein 'the linguistic investigation receives its purpose from conceptual problems of philosophy, not from empirical problems in linguistics' (Hacker 1986:161). Pertinent though these obser-vations are, it is not in the end clear how they let Wittgenstein off the hook. To be sure, we can if we wish *stipulate* that science and philosophy do not overlap, that there is an absolute distinction between conceptual and empirical questions, and so on. But this is merely to adopt a certain academic stance in the context of twentieth-century Western culture. It is far from self-evident that such a position can claim to be underwritten by any eternal verities about 'the nature of language' or its 'limits'. *Science, philosophy* and *language*, after all, are presumably just words like any others (at least, according to the author of the *Philosophische Untersuchungen*).

Saussure faces the mirror-image of this problem. In effect, like Wittgenstein, he adopts a currently dominant conceptualisation of 'science'. (For any science *S*, it falls to that science to describe the phenomena within its domain, and to explain these phenomena in terms of the general laws of *S*. The way these twin objectives are accomplished defines *S* as a science.) But if linguistics as a science is to be distinct from other forms of inquiry, including philosophy, and also autonomous (as Saussure quite evidently intends), before distinguishing between *faits de langue* and *faits de parole* it must first distinguish *faits de langage* from *faits de logique*. The *Cours* boldly tackles the former problem but is conspicuously silent about the latter. As a result, one is left with a pair of unhappy alternatives. Saussure's silence can be interpreted either as indicating that he supposed that *faits de logique* would eventually emerge as a subset of *faits de langage*; or else as indicating that he supposed that where the boundary lay between *faits de logique* and *faits de langage* could be discovered only by empirical linguistic inquiry.

There are fairly clear indications in the *Cours* that Saussure felt vulnerable to the potential objection that, because of the way he had defined the linguistic sign, his linguistics was only a pseudo-science. In other words, his postulated combinations of *signifiant* and *signifié* did not really exist, but were merely theoretical abstractions, and therefore offered the linguist no basis for genuine empirical propositions. Hence his emphatic insistence that *langue* is not a mere abstraction (CLG:31) but consists of 'concrete entities', even though these entities are not to be confused with the observables of *parole*. The point was a particularly crucial one for Saussure, since he had taken nineteenth-century linguistics to task precisely for inventing linguistic entities which did not exist (languages which remained 'the same' in spite of changing their pronunciation and lexicon; grammatical paradigms which remained 'the same' in spite of losing their flexional distinctions). A science of language, as far as Saussure was concerned, had to deal with linguistic *realia*, not metalinguistic fictions. And yet, as he was forced to admit, linguistics — unlike other sciences — had no object of study 'given in advance': in linguistics 'it is the viewpoint adopted which creates the object' (CLG:23). It is the tension between this admission and the claim to scientific status which is felt constantly throughout the *Cours*.

The ultimate source of the difficulty for both Saussure and Wittgenstein lies in the paradigm of 'science' itself. By presupposing a categorical distinction between empirical propositions and other forms of discourse, it traps any general inquiry into language in a cleft stick. Words are at the same time cultural facts, metalinguistic posits and conceptual tools. Hence to draw the empirical/non-empirical distinction for discourse about language within the framework of that paradigm becomes intrinsically problematic. It involves the paradoxical enterprise of trying to go beyond and yet keep within the limits of language.

With historical hindsight it becomes clear that both Saussure and Wittgenstein were drawn independently to explore the analogies between languages and rule-governed games because that seemed to afford the best way out of a series of linguistic dilemmas posed by the nineteenth-century triumph of positivism in Western academia. Positivist science demanded 'hard facts': but language seemed to offer either none at all or too many. This was a time when the study of language threatened to fragment between disciplines which had little in common: phonetics, psychology, philology, neurophysiology, social anthropology, etc. That fragmentation, pursued in the interests of science and its incessant quest for 'harder' facts, left a disturbing impression that somehow language had slipped through the net of understanding; as when a familiar object, viewed for the first time through a powerful microscope, seems to be no longer 'there', but to have dissolved into a series of quite unfamiliar objects not previously seen. So it was with language in the late nineteenth and early twentieth centuries. The adoption of the games analogy can be seen as a reaction which attempts to vindicate the common-sense view of language in a theoretically defensible form. While not rejecting the microscope of science, it reaffirms and insists that the object under scrutiny is indeed language as familiar to the ordinary language user, the game everybody can play.

At the same time it disabuses us of the misconception that advances in science will of themselves, in time, reveal truths about language which at present lie concealed. To believe that would be as absurd as supposing that future research on the brain or the human nervous system might help us to understand chess any better. Once we see that our mastery of language is like our mastery of a game, we shall reject any temptation to give priority to trying to study it as 'a faculty endowed by nature' (CLG:25), even though it may, like playing games, depend on various naturally endowed abilities.

In this way the games analogy promised that essential *Übersicht* from which it should be possible in principle not so much to identify and order the linguistic facts as to command a clear view of all the various possible orderings and their natural interrelationships. At no earlier period in the history of Western culture would such a seemingly banal analogy have appeared likely to promise *that*. What both Saussure and Wittgenstein mistook for the enlightenment of banging one's head up against the limits of language (PU:119) was perhaps in the end something different: banging their concepts of language up against the limits imposed by a particularly prestigious paradigm of science.

Appendix
Biographical Synopses

Ferdinand-Mongin de Saussure		Ludwig Josef Johann Wittgenstein	
1857	Born Geneva, 26 November		
1875	Studied at University of Geneva		
1876–80	Studied at Leipzig University		
1878	Publication of *Mémoire*		
1880	Moved to Paris		
1881–91	Taught at the Ecole des Hautes Etudes		
1891	Appointed Professor at the University of Geneva	1889	Born Vienna, 26 April
1907–11	Lectured on general linguistics	1908–11	Studied engineering at Manchester University
1913	Died Vufflens, 22 February	1912–13	Studied philosophy at Cambridge
1916	Publication of *Cours de linguistique générale*	1914–18	Served in the Austrian army
		1918–19	Prisoner of war in Italy
		1919–20	Trained as a teacher
		1921	Publication of *Tractatus Logico-Philosophicus*
		1920–6	Schoolmaster in Austria
		1926–8	Designed his sister's house in Vienna
		1929	Returned to Cambridge
		1939	Chair of philosophy at Cambridge
		1947	Resigned
		1951	Died Cambridge, 29 April
		1953	Publication of *Philosophische Untersuchungen*

Ferdinand-Mongin de Saussure (1857–1913)

Saussure was born into a long established Swiss family with an academic tradition, and followed an entirely orthodox academic career throughout the whole of his life. He became curious about questions of etymology as a boy, partly as a result of meeting A. Pictet, the author of *Origines indo-européennes*, who had once been a pupil at the school near Berne which Saussure attended. By the age of 15 he had already written an *Essai sur les langues* which he sent to Pictet, who encouraged him to pursue his philological interests further. After a year at the University of Geneva, he went to Leipzig, then renowned as a centre of linguistic studies.

He first drew the attention of the academic world by publishing, at the age of 21, a *Mémoire sur le système primitif des voyelles dans les langues indo-européennes*. Over the next 30 years he published no other major contribution to his subject. He completed a doctoral thesis on the genitive absolute construction in Sanskrit, and wrote a number of short articles and reviews; but nothing which ever looked likely to change the whole course of academic linguistics, as the *Cours* eventually did. Having finished his studies in Leipzig he moved to Paris, where he soon succeeded Michel Bréal as *maître de conférences* at the Ecole des Hautes Etudes. He lectured on Gothic, Old High German, Greek, Latin and Lithuanian, and became an active member of the Société de Linguistique. His pupils at that time included a number of subsequently distinguished French scholars, among them Darmesteter, Passy, Grammont and Meillet.

On returning to Switzerland in 1891, he settled in Geneva, held a succession of posts at the university, and married the daughter of another long established and prosperous Swiss family. He remained in Geneva for the rest of his career, lecturing mainly on Sanskrit and other Indo-European languages. It was not until the retirement of Joseph Wertheimer in 1905 that Saussure assumed responsibility for courses in general linguistics, of which he gave only three in all, in the years 1907 to 1911. It was the lecture notes taken by his pupils at these three courses which provided the bulk of the material subsequently amalgamated and edited by his colleagues, and published after his death as the *Cours de linguistique générale*. Illness obliged him to give up teaching in 1912 and he died the following year. In 1922 the research Saussure had himself published during his lifetime was brought together in a single volume under the title *Recueil des publications scientifiques de Ferdinand de Saussure.* The original students' notes on which the *Cours* was based were published in 1967–74 in the comprehensive critical edition of the text by Rudolph Engler.

No full-length biography of Saussure has yet appeared. The most comprehensive account of his life available is contained in the 'Notes biographiques et critiques sur F. de Saussure' which appear as an appendix to the 1972 edition of the *Cours* by Tullio de Mauro.

Ludwig Josef Johann Wittgenstein (1889–1951)

Wittgenstein was the youngest son of a prominent Austrian industrialist. The family was of Jewish origin, but Wittgenstein's grandfather had been converted to Protestantism, and his mother was a Roman Catholic. He was educated at home until he was 14, and subsequently went to school in Linz and then to the Technische Hochschule in Berlin-Charlottenburg. In 1908 he went to England and engaged in aeronautical research at Manchester University. In 1912, having become interested in logic and mathematics, he went to Trinity College, Cambridge, studied under Russell, and also attended the lectures of Moore. He returned to Austria at the outbreak of World War I, volunteered for the army, and was eventually taken prisoner in 1918, the year in which he completed the *Tractatus Logico-Philosophicus*. The German text was published in the *Annalen der Natürphilosophie* in 1921, and appeared as a book with an English translation by C. K. Ogden the following year.

After the war Wittgenstein gave up philosophy, gave away a large inherited fortune, and became a village schoolmaster in Austria for several years. He then worked for some time as a monastery gardener, and designed a house for his sister in Vienna. His return to philosophy was in part prompted by the interest taken in the *Tractatus* by members of the Vienna Circle, with whom he was persuaded to discuss his ideas in 1927. In 1929 he went back to Cambridge. In that year he was awarded his Ph.D., submitting the *Tractatus* as his thesis. In 1930 he became a Fellow of Trinity College. In 1931 he began writing what was later published as the *Philosophische Grammatik* (1969). He dictated what was later called the *Blue Book* to his Cambridge class in 1933–4, and the *Brown Book* to two of his pupils during 1934–5. After an unsuccessful revision of the *Brown Book*, he began in 1936 what eventually became the *Philosophische Untersuchungen*. From 1937 he also began writing what later appeared as *Remarks on the Foundations of Mathematics* (1956). His appointment to a chair of philosophy at Cambridge, in succession to Moore, more or less coincided with the outbreak of World War II, during which he worked at various times as a hospital porter and in a medical laboratory. In 1945 he finished the first part of the *Philosophische Untersuchungen*, and in 1946 began work on what was later published as *Bemerkungen über die Philosophie der Psychologie* (1980).

In 1947 he resigned his Cambridge chair and went to live in seclusion in Ireland, where he completed the *Philosophische Untersuchungen*. The last two years of his life were years of illness. He was found to be suffering from cancer, of which he died in 1951. It was only after his death that the publication of his voluminous writings of the previous twenty years began.

Details of Wittgenstein's life are to be found in N. Malcolm, *Ludwig Wittgenstein: A Memoir*, and K. T. Fann (ed.), *Ludwig Wittgenstein: The Man and his Philosophy*.

References

Aarsleff, H. (1982) *From Locke to Saussure*, Athlone, London.

Aristotle (1938) *De Interpretatione*, H. P. Cooke (trans.), Loeb Classical Library, London.

Baker, G. P. and Hacker, P. M. S. (1980) *Wittgenstein: Meaning and Understanding*, Blackwell, Oxford.

—— (1985) *Rules, Grammar and Necessity*, Blackwell, Oxford.

de Mauro, T. (ed.) (1972) *Edition critique du 'Cours de linguistique générale' de F. de Saussure*, Payot, Paris.

Fann, K. T. (ed.) (1967) *Ludwig Wittgenstein: The Man and his Philosophy*, Dell, New York.

Hacker, P. M. S. (1986) *Insight and Illusion*, rev. edn, O.U.P., Oxford.

Harris, R. (1980) *The Language-Makers*, Duckworth, London.

—— (1981) *The Language Myth*, Duckworth, London.

Hovelacque, A. (1877) *La linguistique*, 2nd edn, Reinwald, Paris.

Juliard, P. (1970) *Philosophies of Language in Eighteenth-Century France*, Mouton, The Hague.

Kenny, A. (1973) *Wittgenstein*, Allen Lane, Harmondsworth.

Locke, J. (1706) *An Essay Concerning Human Understanding*, 5th edn, London.

Malcolm, N. (1966) *Ludwig Wittgenstein: A Memoir*, O.U.P., Oxford.

Müller, F. M. (1864) *Lectures on the Science of Language*, vol. 2, Longman, Green, London.

Plato (1926) *Cratylus*, H. N. Fowler (trans.), Loeb Classical Library, London.

Robins, R. H. (1979) *A Short History of Linguistics*, 2nd edn, Longman, London.

Russell, B. (1914) *Our Knowledge of the External World as a Field for Scientific Method in Philosophy*, Open Court, Chicago.

Sweet, H. (1900) *The History of Language*, Dent, London.

Trench, R. C. (1851) *On the Study of Words*, Dent, London.

Whitney, W. D. (1875) *The Life and Growth of Language*, Dell, New York.

Index

Aarsleff, H., 7, 9f.
Aristotle, 27f., 63, 98
associative relations, 23, 58, 84
Augustine, 11, 13, 101f.

Bacon, 3
Baker, G.P., xii, 13f., 26, 50, 66, 105, 112
behaviourism, 35
Bible, 7, 9
Böhme, 9
Bréal, M., 130
Broca, 122

calculus, 37, 40f.
colours, 80
Comparative Philology, 5f., 15f., 39, 63ff., 123
Condillac, 71
convention, 47ff., 53
cookery, 75f., 81

Darmesteter, A., 130
definition, 4, 13, 105ff., 111f., 115, 118f.
de Mauro, T., 121, 131
determinacy, 87
diachronic, 52, 87ff.
Dionysius Thrax, 62, 64
Donatus, 62

Engler, R., 131
Enlightenment, 7f.

family resemblance, 26
Fann, K.T., 132
Farrow, S.J., xii
Frege, 13f., 37

Gill, H.S., xii
Grammont, M., 130

Hacker, P.M.S., xii, 13f., 26, 50, 66f., 100, 105, 112, 124f.

Herder, 71
homonymy, 5
Hovelacque, A., 122

idiosynchronic, 92

James, W., 31
Juliard, P., 8

langage, xiii, 69, 125
language-learning, 13, 14
langue, xiii, 37f., 44, 48ff., 65, 69, 88f., 113, 117f., 123, 125f
Leibniz, 10
linearity, 23, 56
Locke, 10, 98ff., 102, 105f.

Malcolm, N., 132
Meillet, A., 121, 130
modistae, ix, 63
Monboddo, 71
Moore, G.E., 66, 131f.
motivation, 53f.
Müller, F.M., 122

negation, 45
Neogrammarians, 15
Nerlich, B., xii
nomenclaturism, 7f., 14ff., 19f., 24f., 27, 47, 102
nominal essences, 10

Ogden, C.K., 1, 131

parole, xiii, 37f., 44, 48, 65, 72, 88, 94f., 108, 113, 116, 125f.
Passy, P., 130
phonetics, 5, 15, 37, 94, 115, 118
Pictet, A., 130
Plato, 8
Port Royal, ix, 4, 69
Priscian, 62, 69f., 74

Queen Victoria, 8

135

Quintilian, 61

real essences, 10

Robins, R.H., 65
Rousseau, 71
Royal Society, 8
Russell, 13f., 37, 122, 124, 131

Satz, xiii, 69
segregationalism, 113
semiology, xi, 42
signifiant, 28, 33, 81, 94, 108, 111, 126
signifié, 28, 33, 94, 108, 111, 126
speech circuit, 32, 99, 114, 116
Sprache, xiii
structuralism, 43, 65
surrogationalism, 10f., 14, 97f.
Sweet, H., 15

symptoms, 74f.
synchronic, 52, 65, 87ff., 92
syntagmatic relations, 23, 55f., 57ff., 68, 84, 100

Taylor, T.J., xii
telementation, 99
translation, xiii, 44, 93
Trench, R.C., 8

usage, 62f.

value, 23, 28, 43ff., 114
Voltaire, 72
von Wright, G., 2

Waismann, F., 66
Wertheimer, J., 130
Whitney, W.D., 15
writing, 61